THE IMAGE MAKER

edited by Ron Henderson

JOHN KNOX PRESS
Richmond, Virginia

CONTENTS

International Standard Book Number: 0-8042-1971-0
Library of Congress Catalog Card Number: 68-25016
© John Knox Press 1971
Printed in the United States of America

CONTRIBUTORS

RON HENDERSON is coordinator of the annual National Student Film Festival. Former managing editor of *motive* magazine, he reviews films for several periodicals.

AMOS VOGEL, film critic and teacher, who launched the First New York Film Festival nine years ago, is director of the Grove Press Film Division.

TIBOR HIRSCH, a photojournalist from Hungary, has been producing and directing award-winning documentaries in the U.S. since 1964. He lives in New York City.

GORDON HITCHENS, whose special interest is the blacklisting of writers and directors during the McCarthy days, is a filmmaker, editor and teacher. Founder and editor of *Film Comment* for seven years, he has published articles in *Film Culture, Take One, Film Quarterly, Variety, Film News,* and other periodicals.

JAMES D. PASTERNAK, who teaches motion picture production at New York Institute of Photography and lectures at the School of Visual Arts, New York City, is currently writing and directing films and video tape works. His interviews with film directors have appeared in *Film Comment, Film Culture,* and *Boston After Dark.*

F. WILLIAM HOWTON teaches in the department of sociology, City University of New York. He is author of *Functionaries.* His articles on film have been published in *Film Comment* and *Film Society Review.*

ANTONIN LIEHM is a Czech writer and editor who was closely identified with the liberal intellectuals supporting Alexander Dubcek prior to the Russian invasion in August 1968. He is now teaching and writing in New York City.

JULES COHEN is in charge of domestic film syndication for ABC-TV. His articles on film have appeared in *Film Comment* and *Film Society Review.*

JOHN REILLY is co-founder of Global Village, a multi-channel video experience in New York City. A writer, director, and producer, he is assistant professor of Communication Arts, New York Institute of Technology, Old Westbury, Long Island, New York.

PETER SCHILLACI, author of *Movies and Morals* and the soon to be published *Cinema as Cultural Myth,* is a film teacher and critic living in New York City.

AL CARMINES is an award-winning composer and playwright who works out of Greenwich Village's Judson Memorial Church, where he serves as associate minister and director of the arts.

HEYWOOD GOULD is a free-lance writer living in New York. A former reporter for the *New York Post* he has written for film and television. He is the author of a biography of Sir Christopher Wren and the recently published *Diary of a Lapsed Technocrat.*

ALAN CASTY teaches film history and esthetics at UCLA and English at Santa Monica College. His articles on film, drama, and literature have appeared in numerous journals. Among his books are *The Dramatic Art of the Film, The Films of Robert Rossen,* and *Mass Media and Man.*

ANDREW SARRIS is the noted film critic of the *village voice.* He is author of *The American Cinema* and *Confessions of a Cultist.*

ROGER ORTMAYER is director of the division of Church and Culture for the National Council of Churches. His articles on the arts, architecture and film have appeared in numerous magazines.

for the Love Child

Introduction
HATS OFF TO MOVIES

At a time when the apparent demise of Hollywood—the old studio-star system—is being hailed by critics, buffs, and casual moviegoers alike, and the auteur movement is being celebrated for elevating movies from an industry to an art form, numerous books on directors and directing have flooded the market. Although this anthology features interviews with six directors, all distinguished auteurs, as well as essays *about* directors, this book is not dedicated to the creative film author, as important as he is. It is, rather, a tribute to that marvelous enigma, the movies.

One of my fondest childhood memories was going to the movies. With 20 cents in hand—half for admission and half for popcorn (those were indeed the good old days!)—I was off every weekend marquee-hopping. I would choose my film by looking at the picture billboards outside the theater. I never, in those early days, made a choice because of a superstar or a super-director. I was enthralled by, and immersed in, those mysterious moving images which flickered in the darkness. Little did I realize then what enormous influence movies were going to become in all our lives.

The dizzying world of cinema is a child of this century. Its brief history is uneven, chaotic and, some would say, unimpressive. Today Hollywood is a scorned parent which finds itself a casualty of its own kind of generation gap. In many quarters, Hollywood is a pejorative term, symbolizing expensive studio sets, multi-million dollar budgets, superstars, money men, irrelevant commercial products. To the artist, Hollywood is anathema.

In an age of trends and fads, it is clear that we are entering a new era in the history of the motion picture, and the day belongs to the director. The auteur controversy of the '60's is the celebrated phenomenon of the '70's—and happily so, we must add. But in all fairness to Hollywood, nervous and defensive under attack but showing surprising flexibility toward change, the emergence of the director as superstar is as much a trend in the evolution of cinema as the talkie was—and, it goes without saying, as important. Jean Renoir, reflecting in the Pasternak-Howton interview on his long and impressive career as a film director, acknowledges and rejoices in the various "phases" that the motion picture industry has gone

through over the years. He recalls with fondness the Thalberg days—a time for stars and producers and studios. "Life is changing, and an art or industry goes through different phases, and we must accept those phases as they are. . . . I believe that today, fortunately, we are back to the time of the author. I don't know if I can still enjoy that, but I'm happy to see that it's coming, even if for the young ones."

All of which illustrates, perhaps, the late Andre Bazin's observation that "cinema has not yet been invented."

What is cinema? Is it art? Entertainment? Social commentary? *Verité*? Propaganda? Escape? This question was raised implicitly more than a half century ago with the birth of the moving image and it is still being passionately debated today.

Francois Truffaut, one of my favorite auteurs, focuses the dilemma well: "There have been many discussions about what the content of a film should be. Should it limit itself to entertainment or inform the public about the great problems of the day, and I flee such discussions like the plague. I think that every individual should express himself and that all films are useful, be they formalistic or realistic, baroque or engaged, tragic or light, modern or old-fashioned, in color or in black and white, in 35mm or in Super 8, with stars or with unknowns, ambitious or modest. Only the result matters, which is the good the director does himself and the good he does others."

Perhaps cinema is no more than a moving picture which moves people, captures their fantasy lives, makes them laugh or cry, or just diverts them a little. If cinema is no more than that then its *raison d'etre* is justified. But sometimes it is more. Occasionally film mysteriously transcends its own medium, makes contact with life, and illuminates the human condition. When that happens film moves into the realm of art. And film as art is a director's medium.

And who is the director? He is the auteur, the artist whose canvas is celluloid, whose brush is a camera. His aim ranges from Truffaut's "to make daydreams come true," to Renoir's "it all adds up to making your own little contribution to the art of your times." A Jean-Luc Godard or a Mike Nichols are hotter property these days than an Elliott Gould or an Ali McGraw. Joseph Gelmis, in his informative book, *The Film Director as Superstar*, points to the newly acquired importance of the director and the role he plays in shaping not only movies but human sensibility as well: ''We are on the threshold of a technological and esthetic revolution in movies which will inevitably restructure human consciousness and understanding. Accessibility of the means of production and changes in distribution and exhibition will democratize movies so there will be thousands made every year instead of hundreds. And the independent filmmaker, whether he's working in Super 8 or 70mm Panavision, will be the nexus of the change to come.''

This anthology is divided into two sections. The first consists of interviews with six noted directors conducted over the past few years and appearing in print here for the first time. Where necessary, the interview is preceded by a brief introduction which places the director in historical and artistic context. Besides their own works, these directors discuss, often in agonizing terms, how they must work in and deal with an economic and political system which, more times than not, is diametrically opposed to their visions as artists. It is fascinating, for example, to compare the political repression Abraham Polonsky experienced in the United States during the 1940's and '50's, and that experienced by Jaromil Jires in Czechoslovakia today. Or the relative security of an established Ingmar Bergman or Jean Renoir to the precarious new freedom of a Peter Fonda, or the surprising independence of Hungarian Miklos Jancso. The directors interviewed here are as diverse in point-of-view as they are in personality. What they all share is an unabashed love for the medium in which they work.

The second section features six essays, wide ranging in subject matter, but all of them pointing, in their own way, to the role film increasingly plays as Image Maker. More specifically, the essays as a whole explicate how film as a contemporary medium and how the director as artist shape societal values and transform, ever so subtlely, individual consciousness. In fact, it is highly possible, in this electronic age, that the moving image is the single most powerful aspect of our new environment. Highly defined, flexible, capable of reaching mass audiences, the medium of film is representative of the total environment of our time.

The contributors to this volumn are artists in their own rights: filmmakers, critics, film teachers, film editors, and film enthusiasts. Their interviews and their essays do not, happily, present a single point of view. Indeed, the lively dialogue on the question of the nature of cinema, including the related issues of the Hollywood studio vs. the independent filmmaker, artistic vs. commercial and political considerations, the director vs. the producer, is continued here. If there is any consensus among the participants, it is the powerful role film plays, not only in reflecting the world in which we live, but in actually shaping the way we perceive it. Their common denominator: a love for film. Their hope for the future: a revolution in values.

This anthology then, with all its limitations (it makes no claim whatsoever to being definitive), is for the serious students of cinema, for filmmakers, for critics, and for teachers of film. But perhaps even more, it is for the casual moviegoer whose infatuation with Hollywoodian special effects and gimmicks may actually be related to a quest for deeper sources of satisfaction found in the art of film.

Finally, my appreciation to the following persons: To Roger Ortmayer, a sensitive culture critic, who turned me on to the power, potentiality and beauty of film in his classes at Southern Methodist University a decade ago; to B. J. Stiles, a brilliant editor, a keen observer and interpreter of human foibles, a colleague, and a dear friend who, as editor of *motive* magazine, not only tolerated but encouraged my avocation in film while I made my livelihood in the print media as managing editor. (In fact, it was a special *motive* issue devoted to film which led, eventually, to this book.)

Special thanks go to Gordon Hitchens, film editor and teacher whose base is New York City, who provided me with invaluable assistance in the preparation of the manuscript. He produced both printed and visual material and was always available for advice and encouragement.

And last, but not least, to my editor, Davis Yeuell, who suffered through so many ''extension of deadlines'' that, rumor has it, he is, out of sheer frustration, turning in his blue pencil for a Super 8.

I recommend it.

RON HENDERSON

New York City 1971

PART
ONE

1 | ON MIKLOS JANCSO

The Hungarian Miklos Jancso is unquestionably one of the most original film talents to emerge in the last few years. With Skolimowski and Schorm, he is a focal point of the East European film renaissance, where it intersects with growing tendencies in Western contemporary cinema. Jancso's thematic preoccupations and visual style are utterly personal and unique. A poisonous lyricism—anti-romantic and reflective of the truths of the twentieth century—permeates his inexplicable charades of inexorable cruelty, submission, betrayal, and repression, in which victims and oppressors constantly change places and no one remains uncorrupted by the exercise of violence.

Jancso's stylized tragic-epic works have concerned themselves with the problems of power and oppression in images of searing plastic beauty and in sequences of implacable violence and terror set against ominous, brilliant landscapes of the most cruel black and white. These are visual metaphors of truths better expressed obliquely, the anguished statements of a pessimistic humanist, haunted by the problems of totalitarianism, war, and the corruption of power.

Jancso's concern with these topics is obsessive and passionate; he returns to them again and again. *Roundup* (1965) deals with the diabolic entrapment and destruction by psychological and physical torture of a group of 1848 Hungarian nationalists in revolt against the Austro-Hungarian empire; *The Red and the White* (1967) with the endless mutual cruelties and massacres of the 1919 Russian civil war; *Silence and Cry* (1967) with the hunting down of adherents of Bela Kun's abortive Soviet regime in Hungary; *Ah! Ca Ira* (1968) with a confrontation between groups of communist and convent youths in 1947; and *Winter Wind* (1969) with the story of a member of the Ustachis, a Croatian anarchist group of the early 1930's, who is destroyed by the corruption of his group and then is ironically turned into a hero.

Jancso's style—always terse, stylized, and stripped to essentials —has grown more vigorous with every film, until in *Winter Wind* he uses only twelve different camera setups filled with constant choreographic movement. The deceptive simplicity of his work quickly reveals an almost architectonic precision of structure and ideological metaphor; his improvisations are those of an obsessive genius.

—Amos Vogel

Reprinted by permission. Amos Vogel, *Film Festival* ("Winter Wind: An Interview with Miklos Jancso." New York: Grove Press, 1969), p. 7.

MIKLOS JANCSO

Interview

By Tibor Hirsch

H: Very few people in this country have heard of Miklos Jancso *as yet.* Give us a short rundown of your life—where were you . . .

J: And why? I was born near Budapest in 1921. I started in the film business in 1948; I had done other things with my life until then. I am a doctor of law, but I was also studying ethnology, psychology and history of art at the same time. Actually, I wanted to be a theater director but somehow I became a filmmaker. I graduated from the Film Academy in 1951 and I began making newsreels and short films—about 40. I made my first feature length film in 1958.

Those who don't know me well or haven't seen the films can't really tell what I am doing, and can't judge my style. I work very fast. I usually shoot a film in 15, 16 or 17 days. I shot *Sirocco* (*Winter Wind*) in 11 days. I use very long sequences. For instance, there are only about 12 sequences in *Sirocco*, so that some go on for 10 or 11 minutes. I use very long tracking shots. I don't use synchronized cameras and I direct the actors during the shooting. So that what I do is a kind of direct filming, apart from the sound which we record later. In spite of this my films are not neo-realistic but I think they are, as the critics say, symbolic films though to me they are simple stories. Apparently the stories are more philosophical than other film stories and perhaps that is why they are considered symbolic. They are quite violent and bloody, though I am not a naturalist. Perhaps they are a little special, but I couldn't say how they would appear to people on the other side of the world. In most cases, I use some historical facts as an excuse to say something important. They are usually about life and death and take place in wars or war-like situations.

H: Who has influenced you most?

J: Many people, many artists. Film directors and authors and painters. I think I learned the technique of long sequences and a certain dryness in the films from Antonioni. But my films are much more restless than Antonioni's. His sequences are not as long as mine and his films are much calmer. Apparently my last two films have been particularly nervous. There is a kind of dryness in my dialogues, and they have several dimensions so that the dialogue almost appears to be about something other than what is being said. [Gyula] Hernadi [screen writer] and I learned this fairly consciously from Hemingway. These are the people I usually call my "masters" and I usually mention three other directors that I like very much: Bergman, Jean-Luc Godard and Andrej Wajda. I like them all for different reasons. I like Wajda because he is perhaps as romantic as I am; Godard because he is very impertinent—I don't much like his ideas, but I like that kind of direct insolence. He makes films in a completely uninhibited way, and I like that very much. He is like a very self-indulgent child and that is a very big thing in a profession in which one's hands are usually tied by financial and technical conditions. I like Bergman's strange stifled moods which are perhaps a result of his being a Northerner and a Protestant puritan, or whatever it is.

H: Have you seen Bergman's *Shame*?

J: No, I haven't.

H: There is a surprising similarity between *Shame* and *The Red and the White*.

J: I read the story and it's very interesting. It takes place on an island, doesn't it?

H: It is also about a civil war. What astonished me in that film, and also in yours, is a common theme which I think is very important: that it is always the little man who suffers most from war. He is always the one to get trampled.

J: It often happens that way.

H: Have you met any American film directors during your visit to the U.S.?

J: No, I don't socialize much with other directors. I think it's very pleasant to meet with fellow filmmakers, but I don't think it's very productive. One always talks about films and perhaps that is not the only important thing in life.

H: I would like to talk a little about how a film is produced in Hungary. It sounds as though your films are completely private enterprises, the way you talk about the writer, Gyula Hernadi and yourself.

J: Well, that is not quite the case. Of course, Hungary is such a small country and there are so few of us that the whole thing is much more of a family affair. We make about 20 films a year and there are about 30 film directors, I think. These film directors are divided into four creative groups. These groups prepare the scripts but not the Hollywood way where someone is commissioned to write a script, and then you find someone to direct it, and stars and so on; in Hungary the director works on the script with the writer, he also finds the ideas in most cases. The groups accept the shooting script and if it is accepted then the film department of the Ministry of Culture investigates the film from a political and economic point of view and if there is no objection then a certain sum of money is made available. This is usually not enough, so there are 3 or 4 organizations that one can petition for money.

H: What are these organizations?

J: One is a film export company, Hungaro Film; another is an internal finance company; then there is the Film Studio itself which can finance films, and the Ministry itself can give an additional sum to help certain films.

H: How much does it cost to make a film in Hungary?

J: I would say that a film in Hungary costs about $100,000 to make. *The Red and the White* was, of course, financed by two different countries. I couldn't say exactly but I think it cost about $200,000. *Silence and Cry* was the cheapest film. It cost from $40,000 to $60,000. The total film output costs about $2 or $3 million and the films mostly make their money back, abroad and at home included. In fact, all these various institutions come under one heading, including the external and internal finance companies, the laboratory, the studio, and the rest, and they do make their money back and, I think, even make a profit.

H: So you are not employed by anybody?

J: Yes, we all are. Everybody is an employee of the Hungarian Film Studio. We get a monthly salary, but that is not why we make films. Actually, we get this salary anyway, whether we make a film or not. But when we make a film then we get a separate sum.

H: Does this depend on whether the film is a success or not?

J: Yes, it does. When the film has been running for 3 months in the cinemas they estimate the reaction of audience and critics and pay us accordingly. There is a committee for this purpose.

H: When were these creative groups formed?

J: In about 1963.

H: Was the idea taken from Poland?

J: Yes, they are similar to the Polish and Czech systems.

H: And would you say they were a success?

J: Who knows? When the groups were formed, it was hoped that each one would have its own character, but this isn't so.

H: That one would make commercial films and another something else?

J: Not exactly. No one planned them in detail except that people of similar opinions should be grouped together. And that is how it seems to have worked out. For instance, the group I belong to includes mostly people of about my age, who started in the business at about the same time.

H: Why do you post-sync your films?

J: There are technical reasons. I didn't have a light enough camera that was silent and I found that the microphones were not sensitive enough. We still don't have neck mikes. But the main reason is that I constantly talk to the actors during the shooting to direct them, just as the cameraman directs his team, so that when we are doing a tracking shot, we are constantly talking.

They made a film on the set of *Sirocco* and *The Red and the White* to show how we shoot a film. I think it's quite amusing. It's like a madhouse. There are hundreds of us all yelling and screaming so that a synchronized camera would be useless. With this latest film, the French cameraman brought neck mikes with him. The result, when it is clear and you don't hear all of us shouting, is very interesting. It gives a very realistic effect. Maybe I should experiment with this method of filmmaking but I think I would need a special theme. My themes depend on the illusion that there is no filming taking place, like drama or real life. That I am not present with the camera. Perhaps that is why they say my films are so cold. There is a certain restraint in the whole thing. My films all have the same style. If I used direct sound, I would either have to change my

method and not talk to the actors during the shooting, or I would have to use a theme that I am included in, where the audience would know that I am making a film and there would be several transferences of identity.

H: When you shoot, do you set up the scene and then hand it over to the cameraman?

J: No, I don't. Sometimes I look into the camera. I rely on the cameraman for framing. But we more or less work together. We are fairly well coordinated so that I know roughly the point of view of the lens. My last four films were shot in cinemascope. In *Sirocco* and *Silence and Cry* we used a zoom lens throughout the shooting. The camera tracks at the same time as we are using the zoom. It is interesting that the camera can move on a dolly and that the lens moves at the same time in depth. There is another thing: Janos Kende, my cameraman on *Sirocco*, does not use lights except for interiors, and so he can turn the dolly in a complete circle and the spectator gets the effect of spacelessness. We had very long dollies in *Sirocco*, 70 or 80 meters, and we built the sets so that we could go in and out of them on both sides. This gives quite a strange effect. We start from the outside, go in to the set and out again on the other side, then back in again. I think the effect is interesting. And, of course, all this is without cuts.

H: Do you see American films in Hungary? The old ones?

J: Yes. Not just old ones. I can't really tell you. I remember the American version of *War and Peace*. They buy mostly spectacular films like *Cleopatra*. The public seems to prefer this type of film now. This wasn't always the case. I don't blame them. After all, simple people go to the cinema to be entertained and not to think. I am quite liberal about this. Some of my colleagues only believe in art films, but I think all kinds of films have a right to exist. Like literature. There is room for everything: detective stories, historical novels, and also for the experimental works. But in return, I demand to be allowed to do what I want.

H: Do you have a fairly free hand in general?

J: Yes.

H: You mentioned the Ministry of Culture. Who is the Minister?

J: Pal Ilku.

H: The soldier?

J: Well, yes, he used to be the political officer for the whole Hungarian People's Army but he is really a nice fellow. He let us get "arty," as he calls it.

H: In other words, you can make films today other than the ones that serve the "class struggle"?

J: Yes.

H: I would like to ask you about *The Red and the White* which was called in Hungarian *Csillagosok Katonak.*

J: The titles of most of my films are untranslatable. My title for *The Red and the White* is a line from a song, just as the Hungarian title for *The Shining Winds*, and songs are difficult to translate.

H: How did you conceive your idea for *The Red and the White*? Why did you make it?

J: Well, I must tell you that I always say that I will make any film someone gives me the money for. And I am quite serious about this. Gyula Hernadi and I usually have three or four scripts, or ideas for films, at any one time and this just means that if I can't finance one or the other of them, then I go ahead on another one. In the case of *The Red and the White*, I suggested a co-production to the Russians (this was the first Soviet-Hungarian co-production). I proposed four different ideas to them. One was a story about Attila. Then there were two contemporary ideas, one taking place in the Second World War. And the fourth idea was *The Red and the White*. And they chose that. The script was written by Hernadi and myself with the cooperation of a Russian writer.

H: Frankly, I am very surprised that a film such as *The Red and the White* was ever made.

J: Why are you surprised?

H: Well, I am used to seeing the old type of socialist-realist films from The People's Republic of Hungary and I expected one of the Bolshevik military to be the super-hero. Who was the hero actually?

J: Well . . . I don't know. Several people simultaneously, or history itself if you like, or the movement which fought to establish this state (Soviet). There is no super-hero in a conventional storybook sense, just as in *The Roundup* there was no one single hero.

H: Were there any arguments during the shooting of *The Red and the White* about showing the Bolsheviks in a better light?

J: Why, do you think they were not shown in a good light? I think simply that it is a less conventional treatment of a subject, less Hollywood-oriented than films are in general.

H: I wouldn't call it Hollywood-oriented but Zhdanov-oriented.

J: It's all the same. I say this because these socialist-realist films are descended from the Hollywood film which could never exist without showing up the hero in some positive light.

H: Then would you call the Socialist-Realist-Soviet epic *The Fall of Berlin* a Hollywood-type of film?

J: Well, I think that was a bad film. There are parallels to be drawn in many of these films and the heroes of these films. This is probably because most filmgoers expect a story from a film. Most filmgoers expect a more primitive artistic level from films than films are capable of. Film is a fairly primitive art in my opinion. Much more primitive than literature, naturally. It can't be as philosophical, or as deep. But it is not as primitive as certain types of film would indicate, as the typical western, for instance. Every western must have a hero and a villain and a plot that is almost on a children's story level. I think the public is like this all over the world, the Hungarian and the Russian public too, naturally. They expect this primitive kind of film. That's why I say they follow a Hollywood pattern, because it seems that that is where they were invented. Perhaps I am wrong because I am not very knowledgeable about film history, but I think it would be fairly near the truth to say that this phenomenon emanates from Hollywood.

Now the reason why Hernadi and others try to get away from this is partly that we want to show something else about the world in a subjective way. And there is also a selfish intention. No one is going to notice you if you don't do something different. If you do the same as everybody else, then you just blend into the wallpaper. You must go your own way. Unconsciously. This is so in filmmaking and also in other arts. They say that I have developed something, that I have a style of my own. And it may be so if that is what they say.

H: What were you trying to say in *The Red and the White*?

J: Of course what I say will be quite different from what someone who sees the film or a critic might say. Anyway, what I think I am saying in this case is that war and death are the worst things in the world. I am not a religious man so that, to me, life is the high point of man's capabilities, and to die is a terrible thing. In a war or a civil war this is a daily occurrence. I think what I say in the film is that if one must die then one must die for *something*, for a cause, and that this cause should be an honorable one, one that will in some way advance humanity; it should be revolution. Perhaps what I say is a little romantic, but this is why we made the film and I think that perhaps it does say this.

Of course a filmgoer who is not used to this method of thinking will find it difficult to get involved with the film. I admit that. I think *The Red and the White* is a romantic film because I think it says throughout that if one has to use force, revolutionary force, then one must use it so that one risks one's own skin and doesn't send others in one's place. I think one can sympathize with that. If a person risks his life for an ideal. And I think this is the difference between the two viewpoints in *The Red and the White*. The White guards, or the Czarists, on the one hand, are a little like the Nazis were later; that is to say, they act very coldly and get someone else to do their dirty work for them. The Reds, on the other hand, apply the revolutionary terror in such a way that anyone who kills is prepared to be killed himself. But this means that he has given his life for something.

H: How was *The Red and the White* received in Hungary?

J: Well, it got the Hungarian critics' award. Most of the critics liked it. It had an average success. It was seen by about 500,000 people which is average success with this kind of film. One must consider that Hungary is a small country, of course. Some people did attack the film.

H: On what basis?

J: Well, for the reason that you mentioned, that there was no hero, and people complained that it was morbid, that there was a lot of killing for killing's sake, that I repeated myself with these same long sequences. But *The Shining Winds* created an even bigger storm. I was criticized for always using the same long sequences and not discovering something new, that people are always going backwards and forwards, that they aren't in close-up, that I am cold, and not sensitive enough, and so on. *Silence and Cry*, the film made between these other two, was considered a failure. Only some critics praised it and the rest grumbled. Not many people went to see it; it was a strange script. But what is interesting is that despite this the critics and film fans abroad consider it my best film. I can't judge. I just make the films and see them once, so I wouldn't be able to judge.

H: I was often amazed by the cueing which must be very precise for those long sequences.

J: It isn't that precise, to be honest. One of the advantages of this method of shooting is that it always remains fresh. It has been my experience that you can't do more than three takes of a sequence. The fourth or fifth time it gets very stiff. There are cases when we shoot the rehearsal itself. There are sequences in *The Red and the White* and *The Shining Winds* which are actual takes of rehearsals. *Sirocco* has the longest takes of all, so I can tell you about how long they took to prepare. The sequences that run for 10 or 11 minutes take 4 or 5 hours to rehearse, to set up, and so on.

H: Have you worked abroad apart from Russia?

J: No. In Russia the technicians, the camera operator, the chief lighting man, the dolly operators, and so on, were all Hungarians. They work together as a team. It's impossible with foreigners.

H: Why did you take Hungarian actors to Russia with you as you were going to post-sync the film in any case?

J: I don't really know. Hungarian actors play the Hungarian parts. I think it's psychological. If a Russian boy were to play a Hungarian part, it wouldn't feel right to me. Also, I improvise a lot now. There is a lot of improvisation in *The Red and the White*. For instance, the dance in the woods sequence was quite different in the script.

H: What gave you the idea for the dance in the woods in *The Red and the White*? Everyone expected a cruel orgy, and it was surprising to see the scene suddenly develop into a Chekovian still-life.

J: Yes, it became rather nostalgic.

H: And what was so interesting in a Soviet-Hungarian co-production was to see counter-revolutionary White Russian officers portrayed as human beings. Nostalgia is a human sentiment.

J: I think we no longer use the old socialist-realist interpretations. We think this film is in memory of Isaac Babel, the great Russian writer. His short stories are similar in atmosphere to this film and, at one point, I was going to mention him on the credits but it would have been too romantic. But the point about that scene is that I think we no longer think of people or life like that and life is like that.

H: It isn't black and white?

J: No. We know this about the Nazis, for instance. During World War II, the Nazi Gauleiter in Poland was a practicing Catholic, who loved his family, loved music and art, and yet exterminated half of Poland. It's a well-known fact that people are like this. That they are not basically black or white.

H: Another point I would like to make is that in *The Red and the White* the crowd always act so submissive. They are about a thousand strong, yet they let themselves be commanded, herded and executed without putting up a fight, until the last scene at the end of the film.

J: Well, this is so in war. We have a few conservative critics in Hungary, and they attacked me for this same reason. They wanted to have me "portray a more heroic mass."

H: In the last few years here in America, there was strong criticism about the way the Jews in Europe, in Eastern Europe especially, let themselves be slaughtered by the Nazis in a very submissive way.

J: When was America occupied last? What do Americans know about mass-psychology under duress? What do they know about civil war, executions, in a country where the wars were fought always on somebody's else's soil?

H: This might be an interesting theme to make a Jancso film or, as you said before, use a historical theme as a pretext in order to express a contemporary opinion.

J: Did I say that?

H: Yes, you did, in the beginning of our interview.

J: (Smiling) Hmm . . . one day I may cause my own downfall.

2 | ON ABRAHAM POLONSKY

Typically during interviews, Abraham Lincoln Polonsky complains good-naturedly, but with sincerity, that too much emphasis is being placed upon those inevitable questions about blacklisting. Whenever he is queried by journalists about his strange film career and his recent return to Hollywood, they ask: "Who betrayed whom? When? Where? Why those dirty finks and cowards!" Sometimes this kind of interrogation becomes pornography. But politely and briefly, Polonsky answers those questions with a dispassionate candor containing no trace of resentment following his years on the blacklist.

Forgiving without forgetting or fraternizing, Polonsky knows that many self-congratulating liberals were among those informers, surviving collaborators-in-disguise if only by their failure to protest. Slight of build, but a man of reserved strength, Polonsky is sure of himself. He did not then undergo a terrible agony of conscience— whether to confess before HUAC and survive, or keep silent and be blacklisted. Given his nature, he could not have done otherwise but to refuse to cooperate with the investigators. In effect, "I decline, gentlemen." Now, many blacklisted years later, he cannot be smug about having done what for him was perfectly natural.

Simple, yet difficult: I decline, gentlemen. Difficult because there was his slowly built-up career in film at stake, a future with the studios, and the welfare of his family. Or, perhaps more inconvenient than difficult, because it meant packing up and leaving Hollywood. Polonsky, as a writer turned film director, could always return to New York, to writing, to invisibility. Others' names appeared on the screen as authors of his scripts. And there was television. And journalism. And his novels. Polonsky's career as an artist continued even while Hollywood's stopped.

But that is enough about blacklisting, as his films are the main topic. The following interview was tape-recorded in my New York apartment by James D. Pasternak and Prof. F. William Howton. We had preceded the taping by several evenings of Polonsky on film— Robert Rossen's *Body and Soul*, written by Polonsky, and *Force of Evil*, directed by Polonsky and adapted by him from Ira Wolfert's novel. Earlier, we had seen *Tell Them Willie Boy Is Here*, Polonsky's recent film for Universal, in a special screening at the Museum of Modern Art in New York, where Polonsky introduced his film.

The three films above, seen together—and additionally if you include Don Siegel's *Madigan*, for which Polonsky provided the script—make up a related group. The films are basically psychological melodrama. It is a violent, masculine world. The men are locked in a power struggle. The ladies wait upon the decisions of their men. There is a sense of family, or, in the case of *Willie Boy*, of tribe and race. All the films concern crime. Complex characters are found on each side—protagonist *versus* antagonist. Of special interest is a curious ambiguity of relationship by which a man may be the spiritual brother or son of his opponent. These men are drawn to one another, understand one another and try to persuade one another to this or that course. They challenge one another, and then they destroy one another.

Beyond these foreground combats of individual men is, of course, our aggressive, competitive, money-lusting American society. In *Body and Soul*, a Lower East Side slum boy uses his fists to fight his way to the top of the corrupt boxing world; in *Force of Evil*, a driving young attorney uses his talents to protect the numbers racket; in *Willie Boy*, a proud Indian youth outwits but finally dies at the hands of land-grabbing white racists; in *Madigan*, a policeman and a criminal psychopath kill one another, with an admixture of the politics of departmental promotion.

Pride, self-vindication, the assertion of one's manhood—these are recurrent motifs in Polonsky films, qualities that, misdirected, lead the men to destruction. It is this misdirection, or the negative use of potentially positive attributes, that most typifies a Polonsky hero. It is nothing less than man in search of a socially and personally fulfilling use of his manhood.

Gordon Hitchens

Abraham Polonsky

Interview

By James D. Pasternak and F. William Howton

Q: Tell us about your new project.

P: I have three. One of them is *Childhood's End* by Arthur Clarke, which Universal bought for my company to make into film. Another is an original screenplay by me called *Sweet Land*, which Universal bought for my company to do, and a third is one I haven't sold to anyone yet, *Mario the Magician* by Thomas Mann.

Q: You've been working on that property for quite a while now, haven't you?

P: I got it from Thomas Mann in 1950. He was living, in those days, in California. I've known his daughter for a long time, and I'd already directed *Force of Evil*. I got in touch with him and we had a discussion about my notions of directing it, which wasn't to be exactly the way he wrote it. He gave me an option on it, and I went to Europe to try to set up the project, but was unable to raise any money for it. No one was really interested at that time.

Q: Why?

P: In 1950 everybody thought fascism was old hat. I think that was the real reason for it. In any event, when I was blacklisted, I had to drop it. So, the first thing I did, when I got to direct *Willie Boy* and had the project set up at Universal, was to get in touch with Erica Mann, and I got it back. But, of course, in all these years my notion of how it is to be done changed. Fundamentally, it's the same discussion I had with Thomas Mann. It was at that time that Thomas Mann said to me that he thought fascism was coming to the United States and he advised me to leave the country. He said he was going to England, and did in fact go to Switzerland. He had just finished *Faustus*. I disagreed with him and didn't come.

Q: Is *Mario* your most immediate project?

P: I think it is. My problem, of course, is to get it financed without telling them what I'm doing, which is very difficult to do.

Q: Isn't that easier to do, though, because you're dealing with a classic? It has a kind of built-in acceptance for the studio mentality?

P: Well, our studios are not impressed by Thomas Mann.

Q: Yes, but it would make it easier for *you*, an impressive director, to bring in an impressive property. I'm trying to psych out the twisted psyche. . . .

P: They don't have a twisted psyche! Their psyche is extremely clear. There's nothing twisted about studios: They know what business they're in. They don't *understand* what business they're in, but they know what it is. I mean, they don't know how to operate very well, because they have a tendency to make money in the way in which they are accustomed to making money, which is, to do again what has already been successful.

Q: You mean to make a film of the film that was a film originally?

P: It's even worse than *that*! It's to be immediately up to date with what has already gone out of fashion. It's hard to escape that in the studios, because—to use your words—they're trying to psych out the market. And when the market has changed radically, as it has in the last five or six years, I would imagine for them (it has been changing over the years) they keep insisting that that market still exists out there, even when they say, "no, it doesn't really exist any more," we're going to adjust to it. So, now when they say they're going to do youth films, and in a sense are like the people in *Vogue* magazine who have a youth consultant, that's the youth market, this is what youth likes now, then they do youth films, whatever they think youth loves. "Youth" is, of course, a fiction—*their* youth, at least, is a fiction. Actually (they) would like to make pictures that appeal to the television market, that is to say, the widest possible market. They would like every film to appeal to every possible audience. And when they get something like that, they're very happy.

Q: I gather you don't endorse the thesis, which is fashionable, that the big studios' dominance of the industry is somewhat passé, that the success of comparatively low-budget films, medium-low budget films, has been so impressive that the studios are more and more inclined to simply lease out their facilities and not, in fact, the entrepreneurs themselves?

P: Well, that's going on obviously with some of the studios, especially if they're in the stages of potential bankruptcy. But I would say that the new money coming in will ultimately go back into some sort of studio operation, especially if they want to stay in the television business, where you need a studio operation, since films for television and television series are made under studio control, unless you can't make them for the price.

Q: Isn't that how the property of *Willie Boy* was originally conceived by them, as a television film?

P: That was a device. What actually happened was that Jennings Lang, a vice president at Universal, who was in charge of the whole television operation, said that if we brought *Willie Boy* in under television, then he, on his own, could OK going ahead with the project. He was *certain* that if I wrote the script they would turn it into a feature, and as a matter of fact they did at once—the minute I handed them the script.

Q: Mr. Polonsky, could you tell us how you changed your mind? I think you had an original impression of the *Willie Boy* book as being not especially interesting for a screenplay and a movie.

P: There's no particular reason why I should write a western, or any other genre film, although I'm interested in genre films, but I didn't see how it was relevant to me. Not that you only do films that are relevant to yourself when you're trying to make your living as a writer in the film industry, although they do become so. I talked about it with others a little and I suddenly realized that the events in the story had taken the exact sequence of the western myth: the actual historical events had taken that sequence. That interested me.

Q: Which myth? The myth of the western American movie, or the western myth?

P: Oh! The way I always put it is that the western genre film deals with the Western Myth, an illusion. I'd always enjoyed those films myself, as a young man. Now the illusion of the West as a kind of Paradise Lost—in which for a small period Americans lived in this strange and marvelous world, this frontier in which all kinds of heroic sentiments were generated, and in which an idea of what the American was was most clearly presented: the adventurer in search of the Good Life. But, of course, the Paradise Lost was genocide for the Indians, and, in fact, Ford in *Cheyenne Autumn* had that too in effect. But the very great western directors kind of *know* that, even as they're dealing with and eulogizing the myth in terms of its excessive nature.

Q: An exploitation of the myth?

P: Of course. Suddenly, I saw that in fact this myth was still operating—as a notion of American life—and that it was possible to tell the story and set in motion a counter-myth to it. But I wanted the film to have the clarity of a myth and not be overly psychologized, because if you overly psychologize the relation between the characters you destroy the mythic quality in which the events determine what is really going to happen.

Q: Is that why the language is very spare, very lean?

P: And the remarks are kind of gnomic, so to speak—little balls of words like stones and rocks that I dropped. There are only one or two scenes that are really dramatic scenes in a normal motion picture narrative sense. They just drop these words, and they're not very relevant as dialogue, even; in fact, the film could be silent, almost, and still work.

Q: Would you elaborate on the counter-myth theme?

P: The counter-myth is genocide. Now, of course, some of the critics, even those who *loved* my picture, speak of the scene in the poolroom as representing my political opinion, which is absurd, since it's kind of a take-off on a Mark Twain-*Huckleberry Finn* kind of scene in which some of the poolroom hustlers and river characters are making the usual remarks they make in a poolroom. They like

to talk about democracy a lot and what he's really saying, of course, is very funny. When a character says, for example, "Let's hear a cheer for President Taft, but not to me. That's the inequality in the country . . . I pay my taxes," and so on—that's supposed to be a funny scene, and hardly represents any political opinions I might *possibly* hold! I included it really in a way to remind people of Mark Twain.

Q: And also, it's there to give a democratic idea when he speaks of what democracy can do for an Indian.

P: That's right. And it's supposed to be amusing rather than pretentious and important. It's certainly not my idea of what democracy is, if I know what my idea of democracy is. I begin to doubt it occasionally. So, the counter-myth is the genocide theme.

Now, the film is embedded in the whole notion of racism, and it's not against it in any kind of way, as if that were the point of the film. It just takes that for granted. What I do is assume that the western myth is fundamentally racist, even though the question never comes up, but just the way the Indian appears in the mythology of American life: an invisible person. They're the original exiles in this country. And, of course, that third factor came into mind when I finally became interested in it because I've been a kind of invisible exile myself, in my own country, for twenty years.

Q: And you, like Willie Boy, refuse to be invisible.

P: But I was luckier than he was, because I didn't believe in the Indian notion of the earlier days of not commiting suicide, because if you committed suicide, you lost your relationship to whatever future there was after death. So what the Indians did was charge into the enemy and have the enemy kill them so that they died heroically in battle, which is exactly what Willie does on top of the mountain, because he could have killed the sheriff Coop, with any of those three shots which is demonstrated in the attack on the posse.

Q: You wanted to, it seems, say something from your generation's perspective to youth of today through this film that has some relationship to your being blacklisted for twenty years. You have also mentioned that you think of this film as a "free gift" of entertainment. How do you relate these two conceptions of *Willie Boy*?

P: I think it's important to know that, to begin with, I didn't make this film for any market. I assumed in the very beginning, when it became possible to make this film, which was an accident and a miracle of a sort, to get the right to direct a film after twenty years and spend $2,300,000 of their money, it's impossible, and when the impossible occurs, it's like a miracle. So I made this film, with the notion in mind that it was probably unlikely that, first, I would ever finish it, because it's possible you might not finish it, and secondly, I probably wouldn't make another film again as a director, because it's very hard to be a director in Hollywood. The director is the most dangerous man in the business and usually he is circumscribed in various kinds of ways; the old producer-supervisor system was set up to control the director.

Q: You mean from the Thalberg days?

P: Oh, yes, sure. The whole point about it was that the director was an employee, and not the maker of the film. The maker of the film was the producer. Now this has been changing, of course, in recent years, and never was really true; it was true financially, but never was true in the case of the really important directors, because they, in some way, were always making their films, using products, stories, handed to them of which they had very little choice. In a very significant way, they were actually making their films, and there now would be no film history or film classes if they *hadn't* been doing it. You would have had nothing but sociology as a way of studying film. This would have been a product made in those days; it would have had its audience; it was made for this kind of an audience; it was made like *The Saturday Evening Post* stories, or whatever stories were being made then, and when the time passes the product is gone, has been consumed, and can never be reconsumed, because it's so boring, dated, and gone.

Now what makes that not true is the fact that the directors really operated during this period and created the medium as you now know it. Walsh did it, Ford did it, von Stroheim did it, all the ordinary American directors in one form or another did it. In

recent years it's been recognized that this is so and now that they begin to speak of film as an art form, why, of course everybody becomes very self-conscious about that, and begins to make films that reproduce the discoveries made in the other arts—to imitate them, so they feel it's more artistic that way—but fundamentally I would say that the contribution made by the older directors is even more significant in that sense, but they didn't think so. It's better to make movies than works of art.

Q: You said that you spent 20 years directing films in your mind. Surely you must have lived vicariously in the films of others. What filmmakers are you interested in?

P: It's hard for me to remember the films of those 20 years—there are all the American films that were made and all the foreign films that were made. When I made that remark, it was made because I'd been challenged by a peculiar question. The question was in praise of me; it embarrassed me. It went something like this: "How come, after not directing a film for 20 years and having only made one before, this is such a good picture?" I don't know how to answer that question, so what I said was I've been directing films in my mind for 20 years and I've had a lot of experience.

Of course, it's based on another notion which I think I share with some people that being a director is something in your mind and not just a question of techniques. The techniques of directing a film are really trivial, I would say. The techniques are not trivial in the sense that the more experience you have the more valuable your resources are when you begin to approach a subject. That's really true. But you elect yourself to be a director the way you elect yourself to be a writer, or elect yourself to be a revolutionary, or you elect yourself to be a prophet. There's no evidence except the conviction in your own mind and whatever sympathy you feel for works similar to what you have in mind. Having elected yourself, you try to get somebody to let you practice this new profession you've chosen for yourself. If it's a revolutionary, it's a revolution; if it's a director, it's a film; if it's a writer, it's a novel; if it's a painter, it's a picture. Now, there's quite a wasted election from that, naturally, but some are not wasted.

Q: Would you elaborate on what you mean when you say that the technique of directing a film is trivial?

P: There's nothing trivial about the technique; what's trivial is your control over it. In the commercial picture the fundamental resource is the actor. There is enough resource in the studio, if your election is correct, that you are able to draw upon it very freely, and in terms of what your notion of your film is. In the elaboration of all the techniques into film, you are almost able to assume others' talents as your own. That demands a certain kind of temperament, a certain kind of intelligence, a certain talent.

The precondition of a certain kind of elaborate technical training, like the one that makes you a surgeon, is not the same thing that makes you a director. And somewhere along the line before you elect yourself director or get the job, you've done something in film. In my case, I had been a screenwriter. And being a screenwriter is in effect to do all the things you talk about by assuming that someone would show you how to do it if you had to do it. The screenplay is evidently a strategy for making a film.

Q: So on the basis of two films you've learned on the job and you're ready to make your first film?

P: On the basis of my past I am willing to say that I am willing to re-elect myself on the next occasion. I don't know if this makes it clear, but I really think that you can watch a thousand films, if you're a writer, of course, or an editor and have worked on many films, but being a director is a unique kind of thing, like being a novelist or being a painter, and most of us share that unique ability in some sense, but not as much as others.

Q: You wrote *Body and Soul* before you directed *Force of Evil*?

P: Right. *Body and Soul* was a situation where the writer turned out to have more influence with the producer and the studio than the director did, which is very bad for the director, Bob Rossen. But it didn't hurt Rossen because after he made that film, he became an important director.

Q: What were your impressions of Rossen? Did you ever agree on an interpretation?

P: I never interfered, actually, on the interpretation of the movie. We discussed it all the time in the sense that I had opinion, that Rossen had opinions, or anyone else had opinions. That's not interference; it was a normal, healthy situation. The genuine interference that I posed had to do with the fact that Rossen was a writer, and his conceptions of what a scene should be began to alter as he directed the film. He would like to bring out elements that I suppressed, for example.

Q: Like what?

P: Well, I think he is more sentimental than I am, in the main, and also his force comes from the application of a great deal of energy —unrelenting exercise of energy throughout the picture. He was in an unfortunate position because if I hadn't been there, he would have been able to rewrite scenes to make them happen that way. No one would have objected, but with me objecting, he wasn't able to do that.

Q: Isn't it rather atypical for the writer to have as much influence compared to the director as you described?

P: Right. And it happened because of the personal relations that had been established so quickly between Garfield, who played the lead, myself, and Bob Roberts, the producer—between myself and Enterprise Studios which is the very reason that I was able to direct there. In other words, I think it was a question of personality, I suppose—I don't know what the words are for this—it was my relationship to the whole project that gave them the confidence that I could direct.

Q: Did Rossen have another ending he wanted to shoot?

P: Yes. He suggested another ending to the story which was really carrying through my ending which was very ambiguous. Rossen said it should end as a real tragedy, and he wrote such an ending. And we decided to shoot them both because it was the end of the picture. In Rossen's ending Garfield gets shot and rolls through the ashcans, and they fall on top of him, and he's dead among the garbage of history. Then we shot my ending which was more ambigu-

ous, in the sense that Garfield says that everybody dies, and he walks off. He may or may not die, but what's so unusual about that? Everybody may or may not die all the time.

So we screened both versions the next day and Rossen got up and said, "we'll use Polonsky's," and that was the end of it. He agreed. So I would say that in the main our relationship was good, although in memory Rossen probably resented it a lot. But people always resent you when they disagree with you, and they don't win. I suppose that's the normal kind of thing. Anyway, if you've been in politics a little bit, you take it for granted; after all, I'd been a teacher and I was quite used to it. And also, to having my way!

Q: Before we get to Force of Evil, tell us about the group of radical artists you formed while working in the industry during the 1940's.

P: "Radical artists" is wrong, because that means their art was radical, and that's not true. They were a group of social radicals with a rather wide spectrum of opinion with the more traditional Communist Party attitudes as the center of it, in some kind of way, with all kinds of variations all around it: liberal Democrats, Socialists, and so on. That was the community and it was significantly involved in both state and city politics at the time, and I merely dropped into it like I was at home, since I'd been in it to begin with.

Q: Was there a hard-core conservative group of people?

P: There always is. Because the studio represented the same spectrum of American life you found elsewhere. There were conservatives, liberals, radicals, and so on. But there were more radicals than usual in that particular small community, because of the people that had been drawn on for the motion picture industry out of New Deal times. In normal times, it wouldn't be that way, because I don't think that artists are politically more radical than other people in general. They sometimes think they are, but it very often turns out they're not.

I would say that artists—the writers of that time, especially the writers of that time—were more significantly left en masse in Hollywood than later, and even before. You must also remember that the writers had been the leaders in the struggle with the producers in unionization for the writers' union. They had been beaten several times, but finally they won and had a great deal of coherence among themselves. So they were important. In the community. Recently, when I was in France, everybody in Europe wanted to know if there was really a social film movement going on among certain writers and directors which was cut off by the McCarthy movement, and the answer is yes. But it wasn't an esthetic movement in the sense that social realism is an esthetic movement. It was a generalized political awareness existing in a number of people who were trying to make films that reflected this in one way or another when they had an opportunity to do so, but that opportunity in Hollywood is very limited.

Probably the most socially aware films are often made by what could be called conservative directors like Frank Capra, because what we consider socially aware is a sentimental attitude toward the goodness of man, and getting together and working things out right, and getting rid of injustice. That's a political attitude, of course, but it's generalized, like breathing, as opposed to not breathing. It could hardly be called a *definite* political attitude.

Q: You say this movement was cut off. What themes would this movement have brought to the screen if it had not been cut off?

P: I don't know. It's impossible to predict because what cut off the movement was something that was happening elsewhere in the United States on an even larger scale. So that was cut off in the entire United States, which is what we mean by the McCarthy period. You must remember that the main political fight that took place in the United States about this time and toward the last years of the war, and right after it, was a struggle in the trade union movement, the CIO and the structure of the left-wing leadership. And that movement was an enormous movement in American life, and its consequences were fatal because that made it possible for McCarthy to operate against people who lost their allies, because the main allies in that movement, of course, were the organized trade unions, and what had happened during the building of the CIO and all the alliances around that among the bourgeoisie.

But really and truly, the triumph of McCarthyism was in effect the cutting-off of a generalized social movement which began before the war, and identified itself then with the objectives of the war. As the war changed, when it was over, and the battle was drawn between the two victors, that social movement came to an abrupt halt as United States policy changed, and the internal life of the country changed. So the witchhunt against the Hollywood people was, in a sense, a consequence of that generalized defeat, I would say, and it's gotten a lot of attention because everybody knew who these people were.

Q: Do you consider *Force of Evil* an expression of the fear of this movement?

P: Not only that, but an expression of the conflict. Because *Force of Evil* was made during the main rush of that period. The Hollywood Ten had already been in trouble, and we were already conducting campaigns for them. This may be one of the reasons people still look at *Force of Evil* and find something in it, aside from whatever esthetic things they find interesting.

Q: Was the film specifically attacked?

P: No, what they did was attack all the films written by these people regardless of content. They really picked on the ones made during the war period with lines such as "We can get on with the Russians, they're not so bad," like *Mission from Moscow*—a film written by a man who was not even a radical, Howard Koch. But he was blacklisted because of that.

Q: Was there an anticipation of the McCarthy attack?

P: Oh, yes. By the time the war was over, the Hollywood Writers' Mobilization had began to harden its attitudes, too. People who were in it began to drop out. They tried to make films about the returning veteran, his rights, etc. They tried to repeat again the objectives of World War II, the promise to humanity which had been in that, all the usual things, the political hangovers. And the attack had already started because it was going on in the unions. And then, as if to crystalize it in Hollywood, a strike, led by the Conference of Studio Unions, was called which was an attempt to shake off their leadership. That was a very devastating strike because it destroyed almost all the good unions in Hollywood like the story-editors unions. The screenwriters guild, in effect, sided somewhat with the Conference of Studio Unions and when that strike was lost, the leadership in the screenwriters union changed, too.

What I'm trying to say is that you're not dealing with an isolated event in American life, but merely the focus of such an event that happened in Hollywood. It merely reflected what was going on throughout the country.

Hollywood's first reaction to the blacklist, when they subpoened the nineteen (of whom the ten are part), was to react furiously against it. They formed the Committee for the First Amendment, which had almost every single writer, director, and actor in Hollywood on it. But by the time the first hearings were held in Washington—I think by the time that plane got back with them—the Committee for the First Amendment was in a state of absolute disillusion. I went to the various meetings of the Committee, of course, and no one was there at the second meeting. I remember Humprey Bogart walking around the room saying to everybody: "You sold me out! I was in Washington, and you sold me out!" He said, "The hell with all of you. If you don't want to fight, I'll take care of myself!" And he stormed out of the room.

Q: People like John Howard Lawson were such obvious main targets that his jail sentence was inevitable. Could you have played ball and adapted, and compromised?

P: Of course, that was offered to everybody, including John Howard Lawson. People who were more profoundly involved in radical politics than Lawson made the switch, and very often appeared before the committee as what they called "expert witnesses," and made a career of it.

Q: A career?

P: A career of being expert witnesses. They functioned as the main advisors to those committees.

Q: What would you have been required to do and what difference would it have made in your development?

P: They asked me if I would give the names of people I knew had been involved in certain radical activities, and if I would provide those names—they didn't want too many, just a few to establish the fact that I was cooperative—then I could just go on doing what I was doing.

Q: Then you would have continued to get directing offers?

P: Of course, they guaranteed them.

Q: You might have made *Funny Girl*?

P: No, I might have made a whole series of Kazan pictures.

Q: There were others, like Rossen and Kazan, who talked. What were your decisions at the time? Did you talk them over with your wife?

P: It never occurred to me as a possible action. I mean, I never thought of doing that. I knew it existed as a possibility because it had been offered to me, and I had seen it operate around me, but it never even occurred to me, the way it doesn't occur to me to hit you on the head and take your purse. Now, of course, you might say, "what would you do if you were hungry and starving?" Well, our attitude is that nobody should have been hungry and starving in that time because it wasn't that situation. I know from experience and from knowledge that lots of people were forced to talk about their friends when they were captured by the enemy in Germany, Italy, maybe even Russia, too. And did. Some did; some didn't. Just what the limits of resistance are in these cases is doubtful; we don't really know. We just know that some do and some don't. We know that some last longer, and some don't. I don't take any moral position on that because I think to do so is an ungenerous attitude toward the problems of living. Life can be extremely difficult and, at points, people survive under any circumstances they can. It may not be worth surviving, but that's a kind of *post facto* decision that people make, you know.

I don't believe that's a serious judgment to be made on people, when you know all the circumstances of it, even in the case of the people who talked before the Committee. My feeling toward them

is that that they did what I consider a bad thing. I'm sorry they did it, and I'm not interested in being their friends, or anything like that, but people do that in life. People live a long time, and act badly very often. But that should not upset your general attitude toward what should be done.

Q: How can it help then?

P: No, what you do is do what should be done, according to how you conceive how things should be done, if that's the kind of thing that interests you. And when some fall off, they fall off, that's all. That's the way it happens. I mean, in the general biology of humanity it's a very common occurrence. Maybe that's the way evolution works, I don't know.

Q: You were natural and spontaneous; it wasn't a matter of ruminating?

P: No, when you start to ruminate, you get into trouble. If you start to ruminate on the question of betrayal, you are in the process of betraying, very often. You don't necessarily have to do so, and may not, but then you have a lot of self-punishment and self-pity going on all the time. And that's the worst form of punishment the enemy can accomplish, I guess. To make you think, my God, how good things would have been, if I'd only cooperated! What a lifetime of punishment that must be.

Q: You mentioned the price paid by the people who cooperated; but didn't you pay a price, too? You referred on another occasion to working on "rotten pictures" for TV or for Hollywood. This must have been an unpleasant experience.

P: You're assuming that we did nothing else. In any case, I wrote books, I wrote articles, I carried a picket sign against the Korean War, I continued to live in a more general way than just being a writer working in Hollywood, as I do now. So the life wasn't that narrow and sterile. You see, a whole life went on at the same time in every sense of the word. That's why you just don't make a film, you live it, too. You're making a film and all the while you're watching to see if it happens.

Q: Do you find it ironical that you went out of filmmaking, at least in the official sense, at the beginning of the McCarthy era, and now you're coming back with a big bang at the time we seem to be moving into a new period of repression?

P: It doesn't strike me as ironical at all. It strikes me as significant. What I mean: I feel like a judoscope.

Q: I'm not sure you want to comment on this, but at present the attacks on the mass media by Agnew, and the deliberate use of the mass media, especially television, by Nixon, suggests to many people that a new version of McCarthyism is building up which will take as its focus of interest the writers and artists and producers in the mass media. Do you see it that way?

P: You must remember that Nixon was one of the main McCarthyites. It was Nixon who red-baited Helen Gahagan Douglas out of her job in Congress, and he made his career in Washington as such a person; now he's the President of the United States. He's just changed his advertising agency, that's all, not his opinions. I agree with the New Left: I think there's a wider blacklist now than there was then. While I was in Europe, I remember reading an editorial in the New York *Times* on the existence of a blacklist in the Department of Health, Education and Welfare. It's obviously true that if you are in the peace movement today, you get arrested, they take your picture; if you're a physicist or a scientist, you can't get a job in any place that has anything to do with government contracts. I think Agnew's attack is characteristic of such a period, and I think the fact that the networks are laying down in front of it is very recognizable to me.

Q: I find it interesting that both of your films, *Force of Evil* and *Willie Boy*, are derived from the two essentially American film genres.

P: See, I think genre, like other social habits, speak for us in terms of summaries of the way we see life. We live out the genres as we live out the myths and rituals, because that's the way we systematize our relationship to society and our relationship to other people. I think anthropologically speaking it has very deep connections with the role of religion in life. I would assume that I am essentially a religious person of some sort, at least in the sense that I try to make things signify as if there were some ultimate significance all the time—the ultimate significance sometimes being something that's not so ultimate after all. That's a question of temperament, personality, belief, and so on. I like gravitation—it's the gravitation that operates when I select themes, characters, meanings, and stories. And I am going to assume without deciding on it, that that'll probably happen with everything I do one way or another.

I don't think that the development of genres in the art forms are accidents. I think they're fundamental to the way art operates on our life. I don't think I make works of art in any deliberate sense —like I'm going to make an artistic film. I don't think that way. But, for instance, if I were to make a film outside the commercial media, inexpensively, you know, about some little thing, intended for a different kind of audience, or a smaller audience, it would then adopt a genre of whatever art form appealed to a smaller audience.

So in the long run, they're inescapable. Now, always, of course, as art advances, what you do is destroy the genre in one form or another, and reconstruct it in some other form, ultimately. If we leave out faddism, since by nature I'm not attracted to fads, and reject them deliberately. But genre is not a fad.

Q: *Force of Evil* is essentially a study of polarities. You have an evil man who is a little man and you have an even more evil man who's a big man, and in between you have a fat, heart-aching slob, Leo. Did you mean Leo to be humanity, torn in between and unable to make a decision, helpless in the midst of all these forces at work?

P: Well, I don't think he's a slob, because I don't think that about humanity, of course. But I do think that most of us are able to work out a pattern of behavior in society in which we can accept a role we don't want to play in general for the benefits we get immediately by not recognizing what the implications are. So, Leo is able to say, ''Gee, I just run a small business, I'm good to my help, it's not really a bad thing I'm doing, everybody depends on me, and now you want to get me involved with something big and terrible'' because he doesn't realize that that relationship is inevitable. And his brother's superiority to him as a person or as an intellectual is that he knows that you can't be slightly pregnant with evil in this society, you're dealing with it all the time, it's part of your life, and it's manipulating you as you think you're manipulating it. So Joe, in effect says, "Let's manipulate it and let's beat it, and take the advantages," and his brother says, "You'll become an evil man. You'll be Cain. You'll be a murderer." And Joe says, "I'm not the murderer, the whole thing is the murderer and we don't have much choice anyhow, so let's beat it. We have to survive. Let's be on top instead of on the bottom, because on the bottom you're doing the same thing, except it's doing it more to you than you to it." This relativity in values, which to each of the people seems to be ultimate, are fundamentally not ultimates at all, and this relativity of values is coextensive with the entire morality of our society, I would say. And all societies, perhaps, I don't know, except the one we hope someday will come, which will not be like that.

Q: I find it interesting that the flaw in Joe's development as a fictional character is his desire to maintain the sense of family, to protect his brothers, and it brings his ultimate downfall. In *Willie Boy* you have a hero who refuses to participate in the family relationships of, let's say, a tribal society. And this also brings his downfall. What were you saying in 1948, about families?

P: I've been trying to see some families in 1970. I'm looking very hard, but I can't see any. In the older Jewish environment, the family center was a source of strength, because it formed a cooperative effort in a hostile society. We were able to draw force from it, and allies. The tribal structure of the Indians is a disaster for them today. It's a disaster for the Africans, too, isn't it? Because in the context of modern technology, it has no strength to win. Willie is not a reservation Indian, he's not a white man either, although he's a partial success in the white world. He's a success in the white world by refusing to be white, and he's a success in the Indian world by refusing to be an Indian, and in that sense is able to exist as himself. But the moment the event starts, which he sets off, and he does an Indian thing, he runs off with the girl who's

now his wife, now the old rituals and habits of his particular inherited myth, which is disaster for the Indians, begin to operate. And the more he becomes an Indian, the more impossible it becomes for him to live. And when he's really and truly an Indian in the end, he's like all the Indians, he's dead.

Q: One final question: What advice would you give a young writer-director with ambitions to direct a feature?

P: Don't go to Hollywood. I would give myself the same advice, too!

3 | ON JAROMIL JIRES

The Jaromil Jires interview reflects, to a large extent, the problems of the moment. The Czechoslovak film industry was caught in two traps. On one side, it could not (producing 36 feature films a year and conceiving film as an art) justify economically its existence within the narrow frame of a market in a country with a population of 14 million. It needed the State, its subsidies, its rich and open hand. On the other side, this meant, necessarily, restrictions imposed on the film industry by the State. As any producer, the State required that it get what it paid for. Thus the Czechoslovak filmmakers were looking for another mode which would combine state guarantees with economic independence. This would give more freedom to the filmmakers and, on the other hand, destroy the argument of little or no profit used against the politically and artistically most important of Czech films and directors.

The Russian occupation of Czechoslovakia put an abrupt end to these discussions. The State, the party, the police and, behind them, the occupation power became the only forces to decide and to fix criteria. The result was predictable. Some of the outstanding directors left the country and now work abroad, most as emigres, some with the government's consent: Milos Forman, Ivan Passer, Jan Kadar, Vojtech Jasny, Stanislav Barabas, and Vaclav Taborsky. Others were banned from the studios or not allowed to work at all: Jan Nemec, Jiri Menzel, Pavel Juracek, Ladislav Helge, Ewald Schorm, and Hynek Bocan. Many films produced after the Russian occupation were prohibited and never shown or exported, among them the last ones by Menzel, Bocan, Juracek, and Schorm. Those who try to continue working must film classics, or they switch to cheap entertainment. There is no hope that this situation will change in the near future.

After *The Joke*, Jires started a very different film, a surrealist vampire story (*Valerie*) based on a poetic narration by the great Czech surrealist poet V. Nezval. This project was launched at the height of the greatest possible freedom—the spring of 1968. Jires' choice corresponded to what many of the most committed Czech directors felt at the moment: We did what we had to do, we helped defrost the social situation with our politically and socially oriented films; the rest is the task of the politicians, and we feel free to shoot poetic films about private, individual problems.

In a paradoxical way, Antonin Masa, whom Jires refers to as the one who has switched to poetic noncommitted themes, directed in the spring of 1968 a political film (*Looking Back*) about the Stalin era and has now been banned from work too.

Jires' *Valerie* had an odd destiny. It was still sent to the Bergamo (Italy) Film Festival and won the Grand Prize. Then it was heavily criticized by the Czech press exactly for having been so successful and was never released in Czechoslovakia. (Rights to *Valerie* have been purchased in the U.S. and the film may be released here soon.)

Today Jires is looking for a fairy tale or a classic which would allow him to work again in the Czech studios.

—Antonin J. Liehm

Jaromil Jires

Interview

By Jules Cohen

C: What is the outlook for your production in Czechoslovakia right now? We have heard that the situation in Prague is pretty difficult, that they're tightening up the economic restrictions on the industry.

J: We are stressing the economic situation. The questions of art are going out the window. In America there is a strong difference between the commercial production in Hollywood and, on the other side, the almost dogmatic non-commercial productions like the Underground Cinema. In our country, the process, the evolution of these two great approaches, will be going another way. There is a big stress on economy, and the art of the film is going to play a secondary role. The biggest objections from the Party and the Government against the new filmmakers generally is that there is no public for their films, that people just don't want to see them. In this sense, they have very similar views on the situation as the real capitalists.

C: But there's been a substantial influx of foreign money. Haven't these films all made money overseas?

J: It's true, but we sometimes forget it. Our interest is concentrated on the Czech public because the film industry is actually supported by the State, and the State is able to influence production. It is freedom and it is not freedom because the State is the producer and it gives the money with certain conditions. There is constant dialogue between the producers, the State and the filmmaker.

C: Jan Nemec made a speech recently which sounded like he was quite desperate.

J: With him, the situation is much more difficult because he has made several pictures for a very narrow public, and his films go directly into the cinema clubs (film societies) and to the art house public. In my opinion, films are addressed to the average viewer rather than to the more sophisticated public. There should be exceptions to this, of course.

C: I interviewed Elmar Klos and Jan Kadar once before and they spoke of Nemec. They said that he was commercially unsuccessful but that as an artist he must have the materials to work with even if he does not achieve commercial success.

J: There are two sides; one is making money and the other is film as culture or art. These are two different things. If a painter paints a picture, he actually does not make any money by doing it. But he creates culture. Creative people look at film as art and they must keep this opinion. There are other people with quite different views —the producers and the government. The inevitable dialogue, the tension, begins, and the films are the product of this struggle between art and commerce. *Daises* (Vera Chytilova) is a good example: big trouble, big dialogues, and big problems with the Ministry of Culture.

C: After you did an episode from *Pearls on the Ground* (Romance), you had a feature you wanted to make with Arnost Lustig. What happened to that?

J: It's very complicated. It was a very complicated script. It was a form of pro-fascist kitsch. We had screened many feature films and documentaries from the period before the war. We were trying to get a clear picture of fascism in the early stages from these pictures. These films were very convincing and they had certain qualities and it created in me a kind of horror. I was thinking of how powerful film is and how it can actually play with ideas.

C: *Triumph of the Will*, for example?

J: Yes, and Gustave Ucicky's *Heimkehr,* and others. I wanted to create the special paradise and human relationships of a society where everything is very well organized. It was actually some kind of a house for girls and I was trying to describe the love between parents and children, the patriotic feelings—those things which are very positive in people, but under this system. . . .

C: In Germany?

J: Yes, in Germany. It was like it in these films.

C: You can find these qualities in many of the German films made in the middle '30's.

J: I wanted to put it together in this era when people knew for sure that it was quite false, a quite dangerous period. There was no violence, no torture, no cruelty in the film, it was just a lovely picture, but I intended it to be a very ironic film. I didn't want to present these people as enemies, but I was concerned about how this film would affect a contemporary public. I don't want to talk about experiment in film, because I don't believe in it. The piece itself has to be achievement. But in this case, there was a certain experiment from a sociological point of view. Also, I didn't find much sympathy from the production side for this film because they said this kind of story does not make any sense, though it is interesting. I would like to make a similar film one day. I was talking to many German directors, like Helmut Kautner, and they were very enthusiastic about the project, but they didn't think that it would be possible to make it in Germany. But they thought we in Czechoslovakia could make it; there is a meaning in it. So I didn't finish it. Actually, my script was never rejected, but they persuaded me not to do it. I told them, ''This is an experiment. Give me three million krone ($200,000), and I can guarantee you that people will go and see it.'' This was the question; they did not believe that anybody would go and see it. They didn't give me three million krone, and that's the end of the story.

C: What have you done since *Pearls*?

J: *The Joke* in collaboration with a very fine writer named Milan Kundera.

C: Kundera wrote the script for Bocan's *Nobody Laughs Last*, didn't he?

J: Yes, and also the novel that the film was based on.

C: Do you think that there's going to be an end to the entry of new directors into the Czech industry?

J: I would say that the first expansion is over. We have achieved a certain level, but it's very difficult to remain at that level. We know from history that difficulties set in after such achievements, like the death of neo-realism in Italy, the very short period of excellence in Polish films, and the very interesting and very short period of Hungarian films. Now there are two extremes; we will stay out in protest or we will have to conform. In our country, there is a special situation and I strongly believe that I will survive. Art is very fragile and made up of indefinable elements and we have to do everything we can to preserve it. It's very good that in our country there is a deep friendship between the old and the young generation of filmmakers. There is a "gentlemen's agreement" among filmmakers to stick together, and this is very useful.

C: In your films, I detect a preference in the features, for documentary technique over narrative technique. Your eye seems to be basically that of a documentarian.

J: Actually, the form of *Romance* (the episode from *Pearls on the Ground*) is so strictly narrative that I actually cannot accept your assessment.

C: I had more in mind *The First Cry*, actually.

J: In *The First Cry*, I wanted to create fiction with the help of documentary techniques, by integrating them into the dramatic structure of the film.

C: That's interesting, because I personally felt that I knew more about the minor characters whom you looked at than about the main characters, because they're brought out in very vivid cameos and in documentary detail.

J: Actually, the main characters are not terribly realistic. You may feel, probably, that the same happened with the hero in Mr. (Evald) Schorm's film, *Courage for Every Day*. All these characters are used as a cross-point for the narrative's tensions.

C: Antonin Masa seems to feel that the examination of social issues is almost dead and that it's time to move on to something else. Do you agree with that?

J: Masa, at the beginning of his career, was trying very hard to make some kind of social comment in his films; for example, *Wandering*, and the script for *Courage for Every Day*. He wants to have some kind of evolution in himself, and that is probably the reason he now rejects social criticism. I don't think I'd ever like to make a film with as narrow political criteria because these things are always very local in the sense of time and location.

C: The Czech tradition of cinema seems to be closer to the Italian than, for instance, to the French, because it is very rooted in the society.

J: Do you feel that this is a privilege? Do you prefer this type of film?

C: Personally, I prefer it.

J: We can actually see, from Italian pictures, how people in Italy are living whereas, in French pictures, we can see how the directors are living!

C: Don't you think Masa would be much more comfortable in France?

J: Yes, but the paradox is that the films Masa has already made illustrate the fact that he is able to make pictures in the Italian sense but that he probably, or maybe, wouldn't be able to make the other kind. I don't like *Courage for Every Day*. There is a disproportion between the form and the script. The script was much freer, much more poetic, but Schorm's work with actors is very realistic and earthbound, I would say.

C: What foreign films are popular in Czechoslovakia?

J: We buy American films in order to get money. They are usually very successful commercially. I go to the American films very often. I like westerns, such as *High Noon*. *The Magnificent Seven*, for example, was a great success in Prague. I think *Twelve Angry Men* is a very beautiful film, but it was not a commercial success. All of which brings us back to the problem of commercial versus artistic. It takes the same form in Czechoslovakia as it does in the U.S. People are tired and they don't want to concentrate or think about problems, because they work all day and want to get away.

C: Is it really possible for a Czech film to make back its money just in Czechoslovakia?

J: We are such a small country that even if a film is a big success, it still doesn't cover the expense of production. The income derived from imported films and the sale of our films abroad is vital to the economic solvency of our industry. *When the Cat Comes*, by (Vojtech) Jasny, was exchanged for a West German film, *The Treasure of Silver Lake*. This picture made five times more money than *When the Cat Comes*. I know one woman who has seen this film 50 times. When the people look for stupidity, they like to get it in quantity!

4 | ON JEAN RENOIR

Jean Renoir completed his thirty-ninth motion picture, *Le Petit Theatre De Jean Renoir*, in 1970. His first film, *La Fille De L'Eau*, was made in 1924. What comes between is perhaps the most impressive body of filmmaking ever directed by one person. From his French Period, 1924-1940, the outstanding works are *Nana* (1926), *La Chienne* (1931), *Boudu Sauve des Eaux* (1932), *Toni* (1934), *La Grande Illusion* (1937), and *La Regle Du Jeu* (1939); of the American Period: *Swamp Water* (1941), *The Southerner* (1945), *Diary of a Chambermaid* (1946), *The River* (1951), and *The Golden Coach* (1954).

Implicit in a Renoir picture is an awesome reverence for the forces of nature. Man, the creature, never exists independent of his earthly situation. He may be a hero, like the aviator in *La Regle Du Jeu*, who triumphantly flies the Atlantic. But once he touches earth he is de-mythologized, becoming the love-sick, whimpering child again. This fall from great heights, this grounding of false illusion, is a theme often repeated. Boudu, that noble savage, is rescued from drowning in a river and raised to the dizzying complications of civilization. When complication becomes restriction, he jumps back into the river and escapes to freedom.

Nature is an intoxicant, exciting characters to Dionysian excess and self-illumination. In *Le Dejeuner Sur L'Herbe* (1960), the arch-intellectual Professor Alexis falls in love with a simple peasant girl when his picnic is blown into a Bacchanalia. "Down with Science!" cries the Professor. "Happiness is the submission to nature's order." In *La Regle Du Jeu*, "Nature's order" is a hunt, where the killing of game is a pursuit of love. And always nearby is a river, Nature's bloodstream, Renoir's greatest metaphor, sweeping characters to and from themselves, a symbol of acceptance and Hindu consent.

In each Renoir film the drama of character conflict expands into the larger scheme of social contract. In *Diary of a Chambermaid* the murderous butler is destroyed when the whole community rises up to overthrow him. A villain is killed, and democracy triumphs over totalitarianism. In *La Regle Du Jeu* love excites characters to passionate excess, and a hero dies senselessly. The clearly defined roles of master, guest, and servant shift under stress, and centuries of complex social structuring collapse in anarchy. In *La Grande Illusion* a gentleman officer dies while helping his common soldiers to escape to freedom. The chivalry of an age passes as the bourgeoisie rise to power, forced now to establish new social relationships of their own.

The style of a Renoir film is distinguished by its celebration of the actor's expression. Structured improvisation, allowing the actors *to be themselves as others*, determines how the other elements of the picture will be created. The script changes and re-evolves during the shooting. The camera *serves* action, with set-ups placed only after the rehearsal is observed by the technicians. Long shots and deep focus and movement allow the actors to build their moments without interruption. Editing follows the natural progression of the performer.

What results from this collaboration of elements on behalf of the actor's moment is a spontaneous cinema. It holds a documentary spirit which greatly influenced the Italian Neo-Realists, Satyajit Ray, Francois Truffaut, and others. If a Jean Renoir film seems roughly constructed (a frequent criticism), it is because film for Renoir evolves in mysterious and unpredictable ways. It is an actor's cinema, a human vision of individuals who are by definition imperfect.

To be unfinished and incomplete is necessary to a work of art. The public must collaborate and reflect. The more technically advanced we are, the harder it is to create a work of art; too perfect. Art is a springboard for the audience to create.

The following interview was taped in June 1964, in Renoir's Beverly Hills home. It is published here for the first time.

—J. D. P.

Jean Renoir

Interview

By James D. Pasternak

P: Tell me about your last silent film.

R: My last silent film was a light comedy—a military comedy—named *Tire au Flanc*. It is an old French play which is terribly funny —I don't say my picture, but I say the play. It is typically a commercial live comedy for the big public. And it was a very successful film, in spite of the fact that sound was coming.

P: Did you find the transition from silent to sound difficult for you?

R: No, not at all. As a matter of fact, the sound helped me.

P: In what way?

R: I found a certain pleasure in using the sounds. I started to be interested, not so much in words, but in sounds. In the expression of the human being helped by the emission of sounds. The sounds may be a cry, a whisper, perhaps not a word, perhaps not a sentence. To explain myself, I must quote a conversation I had often with the wonderful fellow who played the part of the actor in my picture, *The Lower Depths*. His name was LeVigan. We used to say we should make sound films, but not talking films. We should invent an international language which would be no language at all. The actors would never explain things, but would emit sounds. You know, like a bird has sounds, or a dog: quee-euee, qua-qua, pa-pa, kee-kee, woo-woo, wee-wee. That would be the dialogue. But not at all logically built words and sentences. Of course, that cannot be done. But that was a way to express what we were feeling about sound.

P: Do you think that the sound films today are meeting their fullest potential? We seem to have just these strict, very realistic dialogue films.

R: It's because people are constantly confusing. People are paying too much attention to the plot, to logic, to the logical approach to the making of the film. It is the eternal fight between the intellect and feeling. Probably we need both if we want to do something of certain value, but we must not neglect feeling. The intelligence is taking over all the time. But there is also another thing: the separation between the creation and the execution, which is very wrong. If you want the execution to follow the creation, the creation must be very clear. The creation must be logical. It's why you need a definite language of definite words.

P: The younger French directors today seem to be preoccupied with ego, with projecting their own personalities in a manner of speaking.

R: Yes. That's a very normal reaction against the fact that the author for years was absolutely neglected in the motion picture business. Even in many pictures now, you have no author. You have people working on a certain task. They work together, but you don't feel that it's the work of an author. You replace the actor and nobody will notice it. You replace anybody in the production and nobody will see it, even the writers. The writers write in a certain standard style and it's very difficult, you know, outside of the very good ones, of course. Also the music is standard.

If we follow the history of art since the beginning, great art was always born by a complete mixing between the conception and the creation. By conception, I do not mean the story. The story belongs to everyone. If we take any great art, the art of the theater, for example, the stories are about the same all the time. The stories were repeated at other times by different authors, and finally the one who had genius did well, and that is all. But when we see *Romeo and Juliet* we don't think of the eternal author who came before Shakespeare. We think of Shakespeare.

P: Hunting for a motif, then, is not so important?

R: It is important because, strangely enough, if your motif is not good you are lost. But the *creation* of the motif is not important. What is important is to *choose* the motif.

P: To bring yourself to the motif you take?

R: Yes. What is the motif? The motif is exactly what the landscape

is for the painter. It's not the landscape which makes the painting, it's the painter. But you need the landscape. Even if you are an abstractionist, and even if you don't copy the landscape, you need it.

P: In the New American Cinema, perhaps the preoccupation is totally with landscape—with the abstractions.

R: Yes, very much.

P: Have you seen many of the underground films in this country?

R: I saw a few of them, but not many. I saw, for example, this excellent film about Negro kids in Harlem. The director is a woman. . . .

P: Shirley Clarke? *The Cool World?*

R: Yes. It was very good. I believe such a picture is useful for the American movie industry.

P: What do you mean?

R: It's very useful because what is missing in America is a sense of reality. And when you are Charlie Chaplin you don't need reality to be real. But when you are not Chaplin, reality may help you, and it may help the American director more than any other director in the world. There is in America a certain tradition of hiding reality —of making up reality. For years and years, reality was much too beautiful in American pictures. It had nothing to do with reality. This reality was the reality which was existing in the spirit of the American public. And the filmmakers were giving to the public the reality they wanted. And now, even if you have art pictures and war pictures with people dying—blood, etc.—well, it's another make-up adding reality. Reality has to be recreated, of course, by the author—the world as it is. Photography—pure photography doesn't exist. That's out of the question. Everything must be recreated by an author. But if the author has certain values he gets a certain feeling of reality. After all, what's the main thing great men can do for us? It is to remove what is hiding reality. And we need them because we are too weak to do it ourselves.

P: It's a funny word, "reality."

R: Yes, it is confusing. Perhaps we should say "truth." But reality does exist and doesn't exist. It does exist only if it is recreated by somebody, by an author, by an author who can be named an author. Many people believe that they are authors, but are not authors.

P: Are there authors in Hollywood today?

R: I think so. I believe, for instance, that in the pictures of Mr. Billy Wilder, you feel they are *by* Wilder. There's a certain "Wilder touch" which is obvious.

P: Is this because he writes the film as well as directs it?

R: Probably. But even if he did not write it, his influence would be big enough to give a certain shape, a certain style to his productions.

P: Because he has that much control over the film?

R: Yes, but also because he's got a certain conception about what precisely a film should be, and his conception is strong enough to influence everybody—cameraman, actors, etc.

P: Do you believe that those of your films which were most personal were the result of your collaborating on the script? I know that you preferred writing the script when you could.

R: Well, I couldn't *not* collaborate on a script. And I couldn't for one big reason. I change everything when I'm shooting. I have to improvise. That's my nature. I have to improvise because I probably don't have a big imagination, and when I'm working on a script, or when I'm working on a script with a collaborator, I don't see all sides of the question. Sometimes I realize what the meaning, the deep meaning, of the scene is only when I shoot it. All of a sudden I say, "but this scene seems to be brilliant, seems to be well-written, but doesn't mean anything." I missed the point up to now, and the point is that I see it only because I saw the actors rehearse, and something was sounding forth and you hear it, you know, like a bell with a little crack. Well, you need a bell without a crack. So, you have to relight the scene, or change something, or push the actors in such a manner that the words acted in a certain way mean something else.

P: That calls for an almost supernatural producer, someone who will give you total freedom.

R: Doesn't exist!

P: Doesn't exist?

R: No! He doesn't exist. Now I have a proposition for something very interesting, but you know I cannot work within the frame of a well organized industry.

P: And Hollywood is still too well organized?

R: Perhaps. That's possible. But in Hollywood today you can do very much. Don't forget this: most of the producers are free producers now. They don't work for the studios anymore. The studios just give them money and release the films, and that's all. Hollywood today is probably the best place in the world to make pictures. I would like to make films in Hollywood. I would love to. It is still a wonderful tool, perhaps the best tool in the world, for the making of pictures. The only thing which stops me in Hollywood is the problem of language. You know, in English I have no ability. What I write is not subtle. And it tires me to present a project in English. It's not my language, and to work in a foreign language is not easy.

P: You say that Hollywood is the best tool. But often Hollywood's films are just that—tooled. They're just crafted out.

R: That's true, but sometimes you have a genius. After all, if I'm making pictures now, it's because of the Hollywood pictures. When I was a young man, I used to go to movies very often. And my favorites were the American pictures. I didn't consider the other ones at all. Chaplin, Stroheim, Griffith, they were my masters.

P: And the actor in film?

R: The actor in film? Well, our master—the greatest of us—Mr. Chaplin, is an actor. Stroheim is an actor. *Was*, poor Stroheim!

P: Poor Stroheim?

R: He's dead, and that's too bad.

P: I thought for a second you were referring to his experience in Hollywood.

R: Yes, but after all, no. The possibility for production of Stroheim was finished with the big organization of the industry. You know, it was either Stroheim or Thalberg, two equally talented men. But Stroheim represented the director as I conceive it—exactly. As a matter of fact, when you say that Truffaut, for instance, is free to make a picture the way he wants, that's how Stroheim used to work. The industry has to go through a certain period of organization. And they did, and brilliantly! They gave beautiful products. The comedies by people like Lubitsch, for instance, were magnificent, were brilliant. I believe that today, fortunately, we are back to the time of the author. I don't know if I can still enjoy that, but I'm happy to see that it's coming, even if it's for the young ones.

P: Would you say then, that Thalberg was an Erich Pommer?

R: Yes. And he was also a genius. He had the feeling of what the movies should be in a certain period, in his time.

P: But didn't this hurt some of the directors who might have disagreed with him?

R: I know, but this period was not a period for directors. That was a period for stars and producers. Life is changing, and an art or an industry goes through different phases, and we must accept those phases as they are.

P: What phase are we in now?

R: It is very difficult to forecast the future, but I believe we are coming back to the time of the author, because of the normal reaction against the spirit of the crowd. The crowd was the master for years. The crowd is still the master in politics. But I believe that we have arrived at a certain period where the individual is very important, perhaps too important. As a matter of fact, in certain manifestations the individual is so important that the individual stinks, to my own taste. Sometimes I feel like yelling, "enough with the individual!" Sometimes I feel that I would like to see, but it's impossible because everything comes when it has to come—the question of periods were important in art—but I just wanted to say that sometimes I feel an immense, a fantastic love, a fantastic interest for early ritual art. For African art, which is purely religious, or for the very primitive days of Greek art.

P: Do we need religion in our films today?

R: That I don't know. The period, the very religious period of the Russian Revolution—when I say religious period I mean the period when the revolution was so young that people living in Russia and the world, since they're communists, were devoted to their creed as much as the early Christians were to their creed, got beautiful pictures. A picture like *Potemkin* is certainly very close to a religious picture. I mean that behind such a picture, you feel an absolutely sincere faith. But, should we say belief instead of faith, perhaps?

I wrote something for a religious review not long ago. Just one page. There is now within the frame of the Church, mostly the Roman Catholic Church, a great interest in modern art. The new buildings, the new churches, are extremely modern, designed by very audacious architects. It represents a complete revolution in the idea of the building of churches, statues and symbols. If there is a new religious art, if there must be a new religious art, it has to be connected with the rest of life. And this religious art can exist only after a certain religious revolution is accomplished in the minds of the people. I talked very briefly in this article about what religion was during the Middle Ages, which was a great religious period. Religion then, and even before Christ, was a part of life. Religion was the very thing. Religion was the theatre, music, any form of art. A meal was a religious function; to make a child with your wife was a religious function; to die was a religious function; to be born was a religious function. Religion was the organization of the whole life. Not only the organization, but the feeling, the conception, the understanding, and art. You didn't need the individual; you didn't need the author. You didn't need the author because the conception was so strong. And I believe that this organization gave us, is the reason for, the masterpieces we find when we dig the soil in Greece or in Asia, or anywhere. But today everything is separated.

We live in a time of specialists. Everything is specialization. A man works as a lawyer. When he is in his office, he is a lawyer, and a very good lawyer, and he doesn't think of anything else. He is trying to help his clients; he is trying to be a good lawyer. Then he breaks for lunch with friends and they're interested in certain sport. He becomes a sportsman. He is exclusively a sportsman during the lunch. In the evening he will be the good father and the good husband. The little wife will come: a little kiss, a drink, you know, the children: how is the school? the children were good in school, yes— the father. In religion, every Sunday (or every Saturday if he's Jewish), he's a religious man. All of a sudden he turns a page, he forgets exactly all the rest, and he becomes religious—and deeply religious! During half an hour, one hour, he's a religious man. In the early days of any religion, that was absolutely different. Life was a whole: including religion, including lovemaking, including the meals, including making a living. Everything was together, and that's very different. It's why we cannot hope to remake the masterpieces of the Middle Ages because they belong to a period when the organization of life was different.

P: Is that to say that our masterpieces won't be as good as the masterpieces of the Middle Ages?

R: No! It's why the individual, the author, slowly replaces the general conception due to religion. And I believe that now our only hope is man, is the author.

P: And the author is really, so to speak, a man of God.

R: He is a man of God. No doubt. But, you know, the author has a terrible responsibility today. Terrible! The responsibility of somebody making a statue during the Middle Ages was very little. The statue was a part of his life. The making of a religious gesture for the sculptor was the same as preparing the bread for the wife. But today the author is a specialist, and to me what is difficult is to see how many functions a specialist should take. And I believe that the only way to give the specialist a certain importance is to give him many functions. By many functions I mean, for instance, in the movies to make him the producer, the writer, the author, and frequently the actor.

P: You've seen many of Bergman's films, I'm sure. Here is religiousness in the most literal sense of the word.

R: Yes, exactly. But a very special religion. It is puritanism, but a puritanism that is very interesting. We must not discard puritanism from the reasons for the quality of the early American pictures. The early American pictures were perfectly puritanical, and they were great.

P: How do you mean puritanical?

R: I'll give you an example. The way love, physical or spiritual, was treated in American pictures. I mean the love of a young man for a young girl, or of a young girl for a young man—the way it was treated. You had the feeling that before the young girl could join the young boy, all the obstacles in a puritanical society were working against this love. They had to fight, and it was very difficult. You know what it was like in a small city: the gossips, the fear of religion, etc. The love affairs in the early American pictures were treated in a very puritanical way, and they were good. They were very good. That helped. That helped Mr. Griffith, for all the love affairs of Mr. Griffith are puritanical, and they are great. They are magnificent.

P: There was this tension. You knew the audience was with them.

R: A tension and a difficulty. The things were not easy. Let's tell the story of a young man and a young girl, and they would like to sleep together. Well, it happens that the young man is a knight in the time of King Arthur. And to conquer the young girl he has to climb a ladder to reach her at the top of a feudal tower. That, to me, is very interesting, because the ladder is very dangerous and there are archers with arrows ready to kill him. Here, you have a story to tell. Now today, where everything is free, you tell the same story— the young man whistles and the young girl is in his bed right away. Well, there is no story.

P: What about the increasing nationalism of films today? Films seem less universal than they were.

R: To become universal is very good; but one must dig the little hole on a certain spot. I know very well that each time (and it happened to me very often) I was confronted with producers who were planning an international picture—a picture which will please in America as well as in Italy—it will always flop. Now when somebody like De Sica makes *The Bicycle Thief,* which is very Italian, purely Italian, it becomes universal.

P: Are we making American films which are really American?

R: The only way for the American film to reconquer the world market would be to make American films—great American films. That doesn't mean that those films shouldn't be done by foreigners. After all, in the history of the American picture, some foreigners like Mr. Chaplin made good American films.

You have to study American society to understand it, and to do what an author should do—to absorb facts, to digest them, and to give them back with a certain order, with a certain style, a mature style. What is art? It is the marriage of the personality of the author and of the stuff he observed. The only way to make great American films is to make films expressing in a genuine way what American life is, what the American preoccupations are. It is possible that the questions are too complex now. There is one thing which makes the making of American films very difficult. It is the fact that a big part of the country is prosperous, and it is very difficult to tell stories about prosperous people. They have no apparent problems. It's why the best American films we see are about the poor parts of America. The poor American should be the hero of the future American film.

P: Why?

R: Because the problems of the poor man are more complex, more intense, more difficult to solve than the problems of a prosperous man.

P: And being a prosperous man, then, is like being bored?

R: Yes. A satirist could make beautiful pictures about bored and rich Americans. That's a kind of satirical possibility. It would be fantastic. My picture, *The Rules of the Game,* could be shot in America today, very well.

P: But would Americans be able to laugh at themselves?

R: That's a different question. I'm not thinking of the success, I'm thinking of the quality of the product.

P: Can the two be separated?

R: Well, of course, if you are not successful, you stop making pictures. That's also something very dangerous in picture-making—the

from Renoir's *Grand Illusion*

fact that you must be successful right away. If not, you don't find any money to make other films. And that's bad because in any other art you have the benefit of time. Van Gogh didn't sell one canvas during his life, but today we know that Van Gogh was a great artist.

P: In your early films, your early silent films, some of them weren't successful. Yet you were quite capable of pursuing your artistic goals and creating masterpieces.

R: Well, you know, patience—patience, losing money, luck, all of a sudden somebody coming: "Would you like to make a picture?" You don't know why. I was lucky during my life, very lucky. And always from people who wanted to work with me. I was also helped very often by the actors.

P: You mean important actors?

R: Yes, for instance, with *Grand Illusion*. Much of the opportunity to make *Grand Illusion* I owe to Jean Gabin. Jean Gabin was already a big star and he helped me. We peddled *Grand Illusion* in every office of Paris—American companies, French companies, Italian companies—and nobody wanted it. It lasted two years, and Jean Gabin was with me. "I want to play the part." And they said well, a picture with Gabin is very good, but we don't want this story. Finally, I found a man who was not in the movies. He was a gambler and he had won a big amount of money at the stock exchange. And he said, "Well, I don't know what to do with this money. You want to make a picture. Here is the money."

P: What was the first film that you produced as well as directed?

R: *Water Girl.*

P: And that was a successful film?

R: No, I lost money. I lost my own money with it. It was after *Nana* that I started to make a few successful films.

P: *The Little Matchseller* was a successful film, wasn't it?

R: No, it wasn't a successful film, but, you know, I did it with such a little money that it had to find the money back.

P: And your first sound film?

R: *On Purge Bebe.* You know I had very few big productions like *Le Bled,* like *Le Tournoi,* and the producer was afraid I would be too expensive with sound, that I would take too much time. I had to prove that I could make a talking picture without too many expenses, and I picked up a comedy by Feydeau, a wonderful French author and comedian. I took a short play. I took a few young unknown actors, like Fernandel and Michel Simon, and I shot the picture. I wrote the script in six days; I shot the picture in six days; I cut the picture in six days; and after one month the picture was shown at the Gaumont Palace in Paris. It happened that they had a hole; they needed a picture. My picture was ready. They took it, and in one week the cost of the picture was paid.

P: Your father died in 1919, I believe—is that correct? . . .

R: Yes.

P: You were 25 at the time, and I believe you mentioned you were in the trenches when a friend of yours mentioned a Chaplin film you should see. Is this perhaps the point at which you became very interested in films?

R: Oh, yes. That was the beginning. I didn't decide to make pictures right away, but that was the seed.

P: The Chaplin films?

R: Oh yes! I discovered the movies. A wonderful discovery.

P: How did you come to do your first film?

R: I was mixed up with a certain group of people making films, but in those days my real profession was to be a ceramist. That was my first trial after the army. And I did like it very much. But I didn't like the fact that I had to have a certain artistic pretense, if I wanted to sell my products. I hated the word artistic. And I still hate it. I accept it because it's so important. Nowadays everything is artistic. But, in the bottom of my heart, I don't like it. You know, you make things, that's all. And they are good or bad. Or they're an expression of yourself or not, and that's all.

5 | BERGMAN ON BERGMAN

People ask what are my intentions with my films—my aims. It is a difficult and dangerous question, and I usually give an evasive answer: I try to tell about the human condition, the truth as I see it. This answer seems to satisfy everyone, but it is not quite correct. I prefer to describe what I *would like* my aim to be.

There is an old story of how the cathedral of Chartres was struck by lightning and burned to the ground. Then thousands of people came from all points of the compass, like a giant procession of ants, and together they began to rebuild the cathedral on its old site. They worked until the building was completed—master builders, artists, laborers, clowns, noblemen, priests, burghers. But they all remained anonymous, and no one knows to this day who built the cathedral of Chartres.

Regardless of my own beliefs and my own doubts, which are unimportant in this connection, it is my opinion that art lost its basic creative drive the moment it was separated from worship. It severed an umbilical cord and now lives its own sterile life, generating and degenerating itself. In former days the artist remained unknown and his work was to the glory of God. He lived and died without being more or less important than other artisans; "eternal values," "immortality" and "masterpiece" were terms not applicable in his case.

The ability to create was a gift. In such a world flourished invulnerable assurance and natural humility.

Today the individual has become the highest form and the greatest bane of artistic creation. The smallest wound or pain of the ego is examined under a microscope as if it were of eternal importance. The artist considers his isolation, his subjectivity, his individualism almost holy. Thus we finally gather in one large pen, where we stand and bleat about our loneliness without listening to each other and without realizing that we are smothering each other to death. The individualists stare into each other's eyes and yet deny the existence of each other. We walk in circles, so limited by our own anxieties that we can no longer distinguish between true and false, between the gangster's whim and the purest ideal.

Thus if I am asked what I would like the general purpose of my films to be, I would reply that I want to be one of the artists in the cathedral on the great plain. I want to make a dragon's head, an angel, a devil—or perhaps a saint—out of stone. It does not matter which; it is the sense of satisfaction that counts. Regardless of whether I believe or not, whether I am a Christian or not, I would play my part in the collective building of the cathedral.

—Ingmar Bergman

Reprinted by permission. Lars Malmstrom and David Kushner, translators, *Four Screenplays of Ingmar Bergman* (New York: Simon and Schuster, 1960), pp. xxi-xxii.

Ingmar Bergman

Interview

By John Reilly

R: When you make a film, do you make the film consciously for Sweden?

B: Yes. My language is Swedish and my audience is my Swedish people. But I don't think it's so different. When I make a picture I never think about an audience. I want to explain something to somebody. It's a conversation between me and the audience. It's a sort of contact. I want to get into contact with other people and my way of getting contact with other people is my pictures. It's very simple.

R: Bo Widerberg recently said you didn't treat problems relevant to the Swedish society. I asked him what he meant by that and he said when he made *Raven's End,* he had treated a social issue he had criticized you for not attempting.

B: I admire him very much. I think he is a very talented man. If he does the films he wants to do, I don't care. I think I am part, a very small part, of this society, and my way of expressing myself is not going right into social criticism. But, of course, I express the time in which I am living. I am expressing the Sweden of today. But not in a limited way. Not in just this dimension, as he meant it. I think every artist . . . I think Picasso, when he makes his ceramics, expresses something of his time. I never understand this silly way of telling artists what they have to do. Of course, if we don't discuss the artists, what will we discuss? But I think this is very foolish, to tell artists what they have to do and to blame them when they don't do it. I think it is a little bit Russian. You know what they told Shostakovich? I think it was about his fifth symphony or something. It was, "please Mr. Shostakovich, please rewrite part of your symphony. It's not socialistic." I think you can criticize everything, but not the way an artist chooses to work . . . If his approach or his product is not alive, you can criticize him. But if it has some life, if it is a living child of his imagination, I think it is very greedy to criticize him because his child is not the child you expected. It is still a child. It is a living thing.

R: Do you feel there is a "Bergman tradition" in Sweden? This is a term used quite frequently; for instance, critics said Mai Zetterling's film was Bergmanesque. Do you feel conscious of this in Sweden?

B: No, not at all. When I started making my pictures twenty-two to twenty-three years ago, I was very impressed by the French. I was impressed by the films of Carné, and I was impressed by a very good friend of mine who was ten years older—Alf Sjöberg. He creates wonderful scenes. I always admired him very much and I was assistant on one of his pictures. When I started myself I tried to make pictures like him because I admired him. All the young Swedish people like Godard, Malle, and Antonioni. They try to make their pictures like them. Perhaps somebody, without knowing it, likes my way of making pictures and starts making films like mine. And then suddenly you find your own way of making films—your own style. But in the beginning you have no style. Nobody has his own style in the beginning. Because everything in art must grow up from something. Always in art there is something before. There is some sort of tradition. If we believe that we are cut off from the tradition we are being very silly. I am absolutely convinced that nothing in art has grown up from its own roots. It has had its roots in something other than itself.

R: Do you ever become conscious of what other directors are doing? For instance, do you ever wonder how Antonioni is using film language, or syntax, to approach what he is saying?

B: Yes. I am always terribly interested in such artists and I always like to know. I admire Fellini very much. I love him and I love his way of making films. Just his way of handling material. I think it's so wonderful. It's so generous. I love it. It's so warm and enormously generous. And I always see his films four or five times to see how they're made because the first time I am always like a child who just accepts. The second and other times I can start to see how it is made.

But I will never make a Fellini film. I am too old. I have my own way of making films. I have my own style. My style is far away from the Fellini style. But I think we have some sort of very strange contact.

R: I suspect that of the directors we were talking of before, the impact at the moment on some of the younger directors is Godard particularly. How do you regard his films?

B: I only like one of his pictures, *The Married Woman*. I think it was a very warm, sensible, humorous, and strong film. I admire him very much because he goes his own way, and his way of making pictures is to me very strange. I don't understand his pictures. But I like very much that he has his own imagination. He has absolutely his own way. I think he is a genius, a journalistic genius. Yes, he writes with his pictures and I think it's marvelous but I don't understand it.

R: There must be tremendous pressure, particularly when you become successful, to make a film that doesn't come from you but comes from someone else. Do you feel this sort of pressure?

B: Do you know what Goethe said? It's terribly difficult to translate. He said, "please, God, let me scandalize myself in time." It is when you have a success. I think it's much more dangerous for you to have successes than to have failures. If you are very young and have success it's most dangerous. If you are older and have success I think it's necessary and very good, sometimes, because you know what it is worth. I always think, "good heavens, give me always some real failures to brush myself up." Do you understand what I mean? For an artist it's terribly difficult to have success always and it's also terribly dangerous to have disasters, catastrophes, scandals, and failures always. But I think it is very good for an artist to sometimes have success, sometimes never be sure. If you build your house and you like your house very much or if you like your sofa too much, when you start your new picture perhaps you think you must make it so you can get another sofa, or at least so that you can still have the sofa. You should think only of your picture, not your sofa, your children, your wife, or anything else. It's very comfortable to have the sofa. You can like it as long as you have it but not be imprisoned by it. Your loyalty is to your work. You can love people, children, women, sofas, houses, and everything. You have to have things you can love—things and human beings. You must know that one day you perhaps must go away from things you love because they have imprisoned you. I think it is very simple. It's just an experience. Perhaps one day you have to leave picture-making too, because you have nothing more to say.

R: Perhaps we can talk about the way you approach a film.

B: It's very difficult to talk about a film I'm just preparing because I want to be away from it. You can discuss technical details, but what it is about, that is very difficult, because you have written it and you have to transform yourself from a writer to a director. When you start directing it you have to forget that you have written it. If you remember too much that you have written it you can suddenly feel very ashamed or very frightened, so I think you have to be far away from the work, between writing and directing. Not think too much about it. When I write the script I always have some sort of feeling, some sort of picture inside. I feel the tensions and everything. A week or two before the shooting I start to re-read the script and often the pictures have changed and have another dimension; since I have written it I can't understand why I have written it, so it's very difficult. I haven't started yet to re-read the script.

R: When you film a scene, do you have a script concerned with every movement of the actor, or do you evolve some of this from the situation as you shoot?

B: I have always prepared very closely. I hate to come to the set without preparations. It is impossible for me, but if I have prepared and learned my lesson very well, I can go away secure, ready to make another scene. If not, if I haven't prepared, I can't go away from the script. I have to prepare before I shoot.

R: When you shoot a scene do you allow for different angles, positions of the camera, that you might wish to add later?

B: Never. I hate that. I don't want to have the possibility to choose when I am cutting the picture. When I sit down to cut it, it's a sport.

The choice must be made before in the studio. I never like to make the choice afterwards.

R: Do you find yourself re-writing sequences when you actually start to film?

B: No. Perhaps I cut out some sequences. You always write too much and it's very good to have too much material and then take it away. But when the actors are there, you get the contact with the actors.

R: You reshot a large segment of *Persona* when you changed locations. Was this because you had changed your mind about the script or simply found a better place to shoot?

B: Yes. *Persona* was a very strange thing because I wrote the script without thinking of anything. I just wrote it and it was very complicated for me to understand what I had written. I had to reshoot some scenes two or three times before when I was on location. We made it once again and that time I thought it was all right. That was very complicated. But it was charming and nice because there were just two actors and it did not cost too much. I did not feel too guilty. You always feel it's not your money—not my money. I don't spend my money. I spend the money of the company. When I was young they always told me that I spent company money and now I think there's still a little guilt.

R: You could, I'm sure, if you choose, make a film in the United States with a much larger budget. You don't feel restricted in any way by. . . .?

B: No at all. I am absolutely free. I like very much to be limited. I like the limits of the Swedish costs. I like to know if a film costs about one million crowns ($250,000). I think we will get it back and that's a very good feeling.

R: Have you concerned yourself with the economics of your films? Do you feel it's important for your films to make money in Sweden?

B: Yes. Why not? Of course I am very interested that my pictures not only make money but that people will see my pictures. But the angles are different. Sometimes the points of view are different.

When I made *The Communicants (Winter Light)* or *Persona* or *The Silence,* I said to myself, "not many people will go from their homes when there is snow to see these pictures." When I made other pictures I felt very unsatisfied or very disappointed if people didn't see them.

R: Why did you have someone else do the script of *The Virgin Spring* and *Brink of Life*?

B: I think I was lazy. I liked the writer who wrote the scripts. I felt good contact and we liked the scenes very much. And I was lazy.

R: You said once writing was a very difficult period for you.

B: Very boring. Because to dream is not difficult but to put it in words is very boring. I don't like the words. I always feel them unsatisfying.

R: That sounds a little strange coming from a person who started expressing himself in writing.

B: It is always the same thing. If you sit down after dinner you can listen to a concert on records or watch *The Long Hot Summer* on T.V. Of course, you sit down and see *The Long Hot Summer*. Instead of reading a theosophic book you watch television because everything for your eyes is more fascinating than reading or using words.

R: Have you ever directed any of your writings in the theater?

B: Yes. When I was very young, but never more. It was terrible to sit, day after day. It was a terrible thing.

R: How do you mean that?

B: I can't explain. But I don't like it. You have to be very careful with actors. For me, at the theater, the actors are secure because they know, if I can't make it today I can make it tomorrow or next week. It doesn't matter. The only thing we need is patience. On the set and in the studio we have no time; we have to get it just this moment. They have to jump over so many steps in the creative process so you have to be very careful to practice some sort of technique. I have my technique and Bo Widerberg has his technique.

He always wants to approach reality and I admire his ambition very much. I feel that it's absolutely impossible to catch reality. It's much better to take a mirror and try to choose a very small part of reality and express it with stylization. I can never use non-professionals. Bo Widerberg often uses non-professional actors in his films in order to avoid the need to "return" theater actors in a film acting style. I always have to use actors. I can't use other people because the real moment, for instance, our presence here is full of expressions, tensions, light, and small movements which I can't remake in a studio with anybody. Of course, I can put the camera here and pick up just this moment with the camera.

R: Does your approach to theater action differ from your approach to film acting?

B: Yes. Rehearsals are sort of exercises for remaking, which is always a problem at the theater. Every day you make exercises from ten o'clock to two o'clock to prepare the actors for the re-making, so they make exactly the same thing day after day, night after night. That is an absolutely different way of handling the actor. When you are in the studio with the actors it's different because you have to get them to make it now. In this moment. And never more. And I think this way of handling the actors is not very sane. It's insane.

R: When you direct in theater do you feel the contact is perhaps more immediate? Do you feel you are getting stronger contact because it is a live event?

B: No. When I make a film I write it myself. It's a very direct expression of my own dreams and I just tell people about how I feel or what I'm dreaming or what I think. When I direct the theater I always translate what other writers have dreamt or felt. I have to make it so clear and so very much them and not so very much Ingmar Bergman. I have to discipline my own forces to serve them, not myself, and that is very good exercise.

6 | PETER FONDA ON *EASY RIDER*

Interview

Easy Rider, the controversial, highly acclaimed Dennis Hopper-Peter Fonda film, is considered by many as a landmark in modern Hollywood filmmaking. The first of a flood of "road" films, the extraordinary commercial and critical success of *Easy Rider* has opened rigidly controlled studio doors previously inaccessible to many young and talented independent filmmakers, providing them with healthy production budgets and a degree of artistic freedom unheard of in Hollywood for untested directors.

Since *Easy Rider,* both Hopper and Fonda have completed studio-backed features.

In this interview, Peter Fonda discusses the evolution of the *Rider* project from its conception as an idea to its completion as a feature-length film—and its subsequent impact on audiences, young and old.

—R. H.

Q: Was the screenplay worked out very completely or fastidiously, or was it a kind of organic growing thing as you shot it?

F: Both. It was worked out fastidiously so that the bank would have papers to look at and something that looked like dialogue and a script that would have some semblance of structure to follow. Most of it was written in shorthand while we did it. There were some speeches that we followed very closely in the script, e.g., the one about the U.F.O.s and the one about freedom. Most of the time we would go into a scene knowing what we wanted to do and work around the schedule that way. Of course, there weren't too many dialogue sequences anyway so that wasn't really too much of a problem.

Q: Did you intend for the religious level to be there?

F: Yes. We intended as many levels as you can find. Dennis was always aware of symbols—religious symbols especially.

Q: Where did Terry Southern fit into the collaboration? Did he travel with you?

F: No. He wrote the title, helped us put it into screenplay form, and he lent us his name to make it easier to get the money. He is a good friend. You see, Dennis and I had never written a screenplay before, so we were unknown writing entities. We wrote the screenplay and Terry's name made the bank believe in it.

Q: Did he write the U.F.O. speech? It sounds so much like Southern.

F: No, that was straight out of Dennis' head. I love to read the reviews. They say, "Terry Southern wrote the whole thing. You can tell by the people in the cafe that they were Southern's lines. . ." And they were all ad lib! All those people in the cafe were just sitting there when we walked in and they began saying, "I think there's some sort of freaks over there . . . You should get a haircut boy . . . I can smell 'em. Can you smell 'em?" And since I smelled like a dead shark I couldn't say anything. You would too if you had been riding a motorcycle throughout the country for six weeks.

Q: How do you think the film will do in the South?

F: I think it will do well. They might not like it all the time but they'll go and see it.

Q: Did you have a great deal of trouble convincing the commercial backers to allow so much artistic freedom?

F: The real surprise was the man who gave us the money, the financier, who later stepped in as executive producer and functioned very well as such—Bert Schneider. He listened to a recording I made. Terry, Dennis and I were in New York trying to write. Finally, I got a tape recorder and I said it to a guy named Michael Cooper, a London cat. I sat him down and told him the story. We recorded the story and then we put it on paper. But the paper was lousy and the recording sounded great so we passed the recording around, and Bert said, "It sounds fine. How much do you want?" Just like that! I couldn't believe it, and I asked, "What do you want?" He said, "I don't want anything." I couldn't believe that either. But he gave us what we wanted and left us totally alone and free to make all our mistakes.

Q: How much film did you shoot?

F: Hopper's first cut was four hours long. It was somewhat of a lyric poem. If you like home movies it would have been fine. But the point was to get it out so that more people could see it, so we brought it down to 94 minutes.

Q: How long was your rough cut?

F: The rough cut was four hours, with a scene missing of 15 minutes from the New Orleans sequence.

Q: I like the way the music and lyrics flow into the dialogue. How did you achieve this?

F: We were very lucky. They were straight off records that were popular at the time. I was very surprised that we were able to get all those record companies and artists, and personal managers and managers in the music industry to agree to this.

Q: There was one line that really puzzled me in the film: at the end you say, "Well, we blew it!" What did you mean?

F: I'd just won $50,000.

Q: Presumably you felt like cocaine sellers?

F: Literally, that's it. When we sold the coke and when we went to buy some it was all over at that point. But we remained obscure so that we could operate at as many levels as possible. I, in fact, personally believe we'd blown it, although I know I'm sitting here now. I still say we've blown it—all of us!

Q: Please explain.

F: The essence of the movie, as far as I'm concerned—at least when I thought about the story, which was in a motel in Toronto—is that it deals with the American Dream, which is "Candy" translated, I guess, into the dreams of most people that I've met, including hard-core communists. Get it all no matter who goes down! The ends justify the means! Make a lot of money no matter who gets hit and then retire! I find this position untenable. First of all, of course, at 29 it is very easy for me to reject retirement, but in any case, I cannot see it as a way to operate this planet, which

is really pretty screwed up. So I want to deal with society and freedom, the individual freedom versus social freedom. I find that we've blown the whole thing: we've blown the Bill of Rights which guarantees the civil rights of everybody who is a citizen of the United States. I look around and find that's not in fact happening.

There are now no brown baby pelicans on the West Coast! You might find this a bit difficult to identify with but they spray D.D.D., D.D.E. and D.D.T. on the plants in California, and it gets into the water, and it goes into the ocean. It doesn't dissipate but stays in the form of chlorate of hydro-carbon. It's eaten by the fish, and the fish in turn are eaten by the pelicans; when the eggs are laid they're so thin in the shells that when the mother sits on them they collapse and are crushed. So there are no baby pelicans at all from Mexico to Alaska. Now this started in 1947. Somebody put this shit in the ground, you understand, for economic gain knowing that something was going to go down—in this case, the baby pelicans. Also napalm, motor cars, all sorts of things, were put together with complete disregard to what was going to happen later because of them; and to the people who are going to use them; and to the environment that has to try to accept them. This is all for the sake of economic gain! That is what the movie is about: by making economic gain, by selling cocaine, somebody's going to get hurt! Of course, we didn't use methradine, which is actually the drug we should have used, because I have a personal thing against it and I didn't want any young bopper feeling that it was all right to use the drug because I was dealing with it in a film. We used cocaine because only the very rich and musicians get into cocaine, but still somebody's going to get a soft head from the coke. So we've made $50,000 on somebody's soft head, which is like Mr. Hearst making a lot of bread and building his house, while he kills a few people, then starts a war. . . .

And then, at the end of the movie, "we're rich! We're retired now in Florida!" That's where we're headed.

Q: But why does the man who sells these drugs say, "we've blown it!"

F: That's why we've blown it! Because by that time he understands that blowing grass, riding a motorcycle, taking LSD in graveyards with hookers, and selling coke have nothing to do with freedom. There's nothing that happens in the film that deals with freedom. It all deals with imprisonment.

Q: Not even the speech about freedom?

F: Okay, that deals with freedom, but actually it is from the point of view of imprisonment.

Q: Do you feel satisfied with that speech against the others?

F: No, not really, because I don't like information in any form. But I find that most people who have difficulty with the film identify readily with Jack Nicholson (the fellow who played that part), and they are sucked right in at that moment. As soon as he walks in and does his number in the jail, you think, "Here's D. H. Lawrence, Indians and all." They're right in there because his character is predictable. You understand, you can identify, whether you're a "head" or straight—you're right there with him. So, of course, he's the first one we kill. It's a dramatic set-up and he's there to give out information and represent the Establishment. He serves a purpose: we give information and don't remain totally obscure. My father saw the film at three and a half hours. He said, "I want to know more about where you were, who you were, where you'd been, where did you get the money to make the cocaine score, where you are going on the trip because I want to go on the trip with you." He knew the story but he was very serious in his criticism of it. I said, "I think it's only important to see who we are and what we're doing, and if you watch who we are and what we're doing you'll see where we go and you'll know what we're about." And he came back a second time and he liked the film. But now I feel funny about the written speeches, except that Jack Nicholson, fine actor as he is, in giving the only speech performance in the film per se, was able to make his U.F.O. speech appear just like another ad lib.

Q: The U.F.O. one, not the freedom one?

F: The freedom speech was in the head but, then again, the symbolism's there. It is so much in the head that I cringe every time

I see it. When I take off my watch and throw it away I really wanted just a throwaway sequence. Dennis was very involved in it when he cut it; he punched right into it and we hit it very hard. There are other symbols that we hit quite hard, e.g., the close-up on the gas tank when I stacked the money in the plastic tube.

Q: Can we hear more about the editing of the film? Where did the sound track come from? Whose idea was it and what sort of trouble did you have with it?

F: We didn't have too many problems with it. It took a long time to get it straight especially from the four hours to the 90 minute cut. We edited 22 weeks—no, we edited more than that for we still tinkered with it several weeks, probably 4 or 5 weeks longer. We had it down to about 98 minutes, then it would go to 110 minutes to 97 minutes—back and forth, as we were juggling scenes, and then we finally cut the music to it.

Q: This business of "flash cutting" in some sequences—can you tell us about this?

F: That was Dennis' idea. Dennis and I agree that dissolves and fades are all triggers that let you off the hook as an audience. If you're fading out a scene the audience knows that the scene is ending and can relax; dissolve has the same effect. Dennis wanted to have some way of dividing the scenes that weren't either a fade or a cut, and thought up these "flash cuts." I was opposed to them because I still prefer direct cuts. I think that both of those times when we cut six frames one scene, six frames the next, then six frames back, six frames the next scene, and so forth, could have been accomplished on a direct cut each time. But it is an interesting thing and Dennis wanted to put it in because it was his gig.

Q: What was your role in the film as producer?

F: The film was my idea and I called Dennis up and asked him if he wanted to direct it and said that I would give him the job. He has an ego like everyone else and would like to be responsible for his own things. Just giving him the job is what I did and that's all. I was just the actor, so I never said "I'm the producer so you

from Hopper's *Easy Rider*

can't shoot the scene." Sometimes I would say to the cameraman, "Let's shoot it one more time," but I often do that as an actor anyway. The director, if he's in tune, will say, "Okay, we'll shoot it one more time." Most of the time he functioned as the director and he was the one who ran the camera. And, we had a very good cameraman, as you've seen—Lazlo Kovacs—and it was quite easy for Dennis to be in the scene. At the end of the scene he would look at Lazlo—and of course, all we were worried about was if the frame was well defined—and if Lazlo liked what he saw it was both thumbs up and we could go on to the next scene. We had a lot of thumbs up! We shot about 127,000 feet of film which is a remarkably large amount of footage. We also shot for 7 weeks and moved from L.A. to New Orleans, which is a long move, and it cost us $375,000. My advice to the movie industry is "try it!"

Q: Was it all shot on 35mm?

F: It was all shot on 35mm except the street scenes in New Orleans—that was on 16mm.

Q: Could you tell us about the "trip" sequence? It was obviously shot with a bug-eyed lens.

F: We had 3 cameras running: a Beaulieu, an Arriflex and an Eclair. We used footage from all of them. We happened to like the bug-eye. It was raining and it looked great. The rain would hit the bug-eye lens and things would happen! We shot 14 hours of that trip. I'm not that happy with the trip sequence, only on a technical basis. Most of it was edged—fogged down—and people were really crushing us. There were two or three thousand people following us. We could have had our own parade but it wasn't really parade time. Everytime we stopped to reload it was a crush. Everybody was trying to touch me, or touch the chick. . . .

Q: There was a moment when Dennis Hopper was stopped by someone and there was a face to face confrontation. What happened?

F: It nearly came to blows. I came along and shook the guy's hand, and everything was fine. What you can do with a handshake! Dennis had bumped into him and spilled some wine on him, and

the guy was already completely ripped. He was coming on and Dennis was saying, "listen man, back off, back off." And the guy said, "you back off, you back off." And I said, "Shake hands," and that was it.

Q: Was it Mardi Gras time, or had you created it?

F: It was all Mardi Gras. We were able to get away with it because nobody saw us. There were so many freaks on the street—all drunk.

Q: What about your single line remarks throughout the film: "It'll be all right" or "We blew it." I can think of five or six different times when you did this. Was there some reason for it in your characterization?

F: I meant to say less than I did. For example, I didn't particularly want to say, in the hippie commune scene, "you're going to make it" because, in fact, I don't think they are going to make it. I don't think communal living is an alternative. It was my intention to say nothing, or as little as possible, and to remain a symbolic character on the level of being there and looking at what is happening.

Q: If you want to remain objective, how do you expect the audience to sympathize with you at the end when you are blown off your bike?

F: Well, I don't expect them to at all. I expect them to partake through me because I didn't say anything. You see if I said everything you could sit back and listen to what I had to say, but if I didn't say anything you'd have to get in there to find out what was happening in my head. I'm trying to make you participate in the first person. And if I give you information, or make long statements, or any kind of character definition, then you are not participating on the first person level. This is why I say very little in the film. Like in the whole sequence in the restaurant, which is four minutes long, I said, "let's flip"—that's all. And we blew it. We blew it because I felt we blew it. At the time I wondered if we blew it with the movie. I'm still not sure.

Q: Why do you work within the industry?

F: Because they've got all the cameras.

PART
TWO

7 | FILM IS ENVIRONMENT

By Peter Schillaci

It would be ironic if Hollywood, after surviving television by joining it, should die a more horrible death: a kind of esthetic gout, an artistic overinflation that set in at the top of the seventies. The signs are there to read. Those preparing the wake point out there is no more money for gigantic productions. *Airport* (which confirms the law—the more stars, the worse the picture) may be the last of its kind. *Patton* is doing well at the box office, but so gigantic a gamble is not likely to be repeated, since the world turns too fast in the three years it takes to shoot such a film. *Hello, Dolly!* was delayed for release so long that some thought it was a re-release. Spectaculars and blockbusters, once the surest money, are now dying from familiar symptoms: alcoholic intoxication with big name stars; cyclamate poisoning from sweet sentimentality; and detergent buildup from hygienically scrubbed plots. It's the age of the slipping masters. The older structures are crumbling, and beautiful downtown Burbank will soon be as deserted as a western street during a shoot-out.

Is it the end of the road for Hollywood as we knew it? If this proves to be the case, it will be because producers and directors have failed to recognize the new role of film as environment. We have to revise our notions of what film is, and learn to see it through the eyes of the young audience that now constitutes the major part of the box office—the sixteen to twenty-four group. This is the group lined up outside *Easy Rider* and *Carnal Knowledge*. These are the people looking for the meaning of recent events in *Medium Cool* (the Chicago Democratic Convention riots), *Alice's Restaurant* (the end of stage one of the hippie movement), and *Woodstock* (the day of peace and love). They are the film generation who identify with the prosecutor in *Z*, with Ben in *The Graduate*, and with the catatonic hero of *End of the Road*. Their new taste is significant not because there are so many of them, but because it portends the future of film art. The young have accepted film as an environment to be worn, one with a different shape than a "movie" movie, and one demanding a mode of attention unique among the arts. They have an appetite for mind-expanding experience, and simultaneity, and their art is film.

How does film suddenly take on a new identity as environment, after only a half century of existence as art? The answer lies in a gradual abandonment of literacy conventions out of which film art grew. Story line, logic and character development are being abandoned (they dot recent film history like corpses in a Spaghetti Western). Critics continue to look for narrative continuity, character consistency, accurate dialogue and dramatic build, and they reject such films as *Fellini Satyricon* and Antonioni's *Zabriskie Point* for lacking these treasured (and predictable) qualities. Audiences, however, in choosing films that leave out sequence or "argument" are opting for film as environment. The screen has, in a sense, less to do with what explodes in the skulls of the audience. The example of *Flicker* made a startling point—the film is in the audience. By reducing content to a flickering white light, the director did not turn audiences off, but on . . . they began to act out spontaneous pantomimes of their own in the strobe-like stylizations of a silent movie. It may be, as pessimists predict, that relentless search for film experience may be reducing the art to stimulation, but I prefer to think that we are moving into an unprecedented level of participation and involvement that makes film environmental art. Young people rap a lot about American violence (*The Wild Bunch*), about radicalization (*Zabriskie Point*), and about racism (*Tell Them Willie Boy Is Here*). A film is no longer a pleasant way to blow an evening.

The multisensory stimulation of film as environment is giving rise to a new kind of attention. We have always realized that film, even silent film, was an appeal to all senses and not merely the eyes. But in saying this, we tended to conceive film as opera, an orchestration of many arts with delights for many senses. It takes several generations to learn how to use the new communications' technologies. The rearview mirror generation gives film book attention, tending to savor and analyze its parts individually, to "put down" the film as one might a book, in order to reflect on how the effects are being created. In this approach, film is almost as private an experience as reading. The critic who watches film only with his colleagues is not merely cutting off experience of the total audience, he is cramping his own experience in a climate heavy with the paraphernalia of print—logical, reflective, judgmental analysis that isolates the senses and paralyzes emotion. Even audiences who are not formulating their review as they watch a film tend to "read" it rather than experience it. This was possible as long as the Hollywood dream factory treated film as an exclusively narrative form, relying heavily on the pre-sale effects of novels for their content.

It was perhaps television that revealed this perceptual set toward film. When the image entered the living room, via TV, people at first hushed everyone who came to worship before the tube, much as one would quiet a film patron who talked during a movie. The transition from film attention to television attention was at least as dramatic as that from book to movie. Only post-literate man knew how to use television as the latest of the environmental arts, a moving image part of the room, to which one may give total or peripheral attention as he pleases. The lights are on, conversation or reading is possible, and the medium is cool enough to allow many activities. The breakthrough in generations came when the kids got their own set, free to develop their own viewing style independently of parental choices, attitudes and comments. This "television nanny" generation does not turn off all its senses, but wanders about the room, bestowing its attention on the TV as a special reward for clever action, unusual dialogue, or above all, commercials. King and not captive, he is, in McLuhan's words, not an audience, but he *gives* an audience to the television screen.

Television has, in turn, freed film. The day-to-day quick journalism of film documentaries has been taken over by the 6 o'clock news, leaving film free to develop documentary as a humanistic art. All the genres now appear on television, relieving films of the responsibility of supplying "chewing gum for the eyes," in the from of "B" western, crime and war films. And television's bland homogenizing of popular issues and pressing problems has opened up the way for films that attack these areas with immediacy, insight and controversial impact. The result is the emergence of a new identity for film.

Among the first of the literary values to be jettisoned by the environmental film is dialogue. The trend is toward self-explanatory images that require little dialogue. The fifties influx of foreign films with subtitles that left out almost one-third of the talk convinced us that in film, as in architecture, "less is more." The works of Fellini, Bergman and Antonioni were not without dialogue, but their images needed no explanations. Like some television series ("Star Trek," for example) which are little more than illustrated radio serials, the old film was with a vengeance a *talking* picture. Fascination with sound renewed dependence on dramatic devices until images played a supportive role. Now, however, what dialogue remains is part of the totality, an element in the multisensory mix. We need only think of the cryptic, computer-like utterances of *2001: A Space Odyssey,* or the almost completely nonverbal central character in the erstwhile TV series, *Then Came Bronson,* to realize what a change has taken place. To complete the picture, Fellini has said that he placed a good part of the sparse dialogue of *Satyricon* in untranslated Latin because almost none of what people say means much in his film. These trends tend to defuse the criticism of inept dialogue in Antonioni's *Zabriskie Point.* The director might well advise us to play the film silently, since it is the images that speak.

Along with dialogue, sequential narrative, dramatic choice, and plot are atrophying rapidly in the new, environmental films. Where there is a "story," it is fragmented intentionally to allow another experience than merely following the narrative. *The Pawnbroker* kept the past in present contexts, exploding like shell fragments in the deadened consciousness of Nazermann. *Petulia* scrambles its story line into an experience that expands from a free-floating present into both past and future simultaneously. Most films, however, abandon story for a mosaic form, loosely held together by free associations and perhaps a central character who does not change

much in the process. 8½ succeeded in unifying its complexities by relating images with no reference to dramatic buildup. Now, Fellini, in his *Satyricon,* merely allows his picaresque prechristian hero to wander through a forest of grotesque human aberrations in his search of experience. Many other films are equally loose: *Medium Cool, Alice's Restaurant, End of the Road.*

Unlike the well-tailored plot, or the tragic-hero drama, such films give only a series of open-ended impressions freely enjoyed by the audience, which nevertheless invite inquiry and stimulate involvement. This is film working as environment, not merely containing but shaping people, altering the balance of their faculties, radically revising the patterns of their perceptions. Ultimately, the environmental film transforms one's views of himself and of all reality. It has been noted before that "grooving," a recently popular idiom, may mean just that . . . a new mode of attention—multi-sensory, total and simultaneous—has arrived. For those over forty, we may warn that, when you "groove," you do not analyze, follow an argument, separate sensations. Rather, you submit to the film (work) and allow it to massage you, hopefully, into a heightened life full of awareness and consciousness that was not previously possible.

Some idea of the "grooving" view of film is provided by the Charles Braverman films, *American Time Capsule* and *World of '68.* The creative fast cutting to which we are conditioned by television commercials (as many as sixty cuts per minute commercial) is accelerated by these films which are under five minutes in length. *American Time Capsule* gives "all" of American history, from paintings, woodcuts, newspaper photos, and film footage, in 3½ minutes. *World of '68* crams all the tumult of one of the most turbulent years in our history into 4½ minutes. Older audiences are troubled by these films, they worry about the subject matter, the emotions evoked, and by the difficulty in physically seeing each of the images, some of which are on the screen only 1/12 of a second. Younger audiences feel a sense of exhilaration. The very act of absorbing images at this incredible rate makes the films a mind-blowing experience, and for each image (many of which we have already seen on television and in magazines) there is an instant emotion. But one does not tick off the events, or see this film frame by frame. The very idea of compressing two hundred years, or 365 days of history into a few minutes is to give under that pressure a sense of major configurations, trends, the "feel" of history, whether our entire past, or our recent present. The use of mostly familiar stills is part of the extraordinary effect of history reexamined. We are invited to review our feelings toward events we may have lived through by telescoping our recollection and recognition of these events. The timing, zooms and scans, drum beat scores and powerful actuality of the films make them something new in film art. What is important, however, is that one must simply open oneself to such a film, and not record and analyze it as it happens. Our capacity to experience such a multiplicity of images is a new one, a learned capacity which has a lot to do with television, and the commercial, in particular. We have a hunger for overload which makes most schooling a bore, chiefly because we feel that our potential is in no way exhausted. Since film provides that overload, it becomes the prime environment for learning not from school, but experience.

Education has come to mean developing the skills for living humanly in the technological culture. But the only way to achieve this is to change with the culture. Most education is involved in the task of prematurely stabilizing change, of labeling, classifying, analyzing and in effect dismissing change as "more of the same." The textbook mentality has meant culling the best of the latest for improving young minds. But no textbook can compete with the latest issue of *Life* magazine, in which the foremost scientific researchers first publish their findings. The media today provide the instant information which alone can keep up with change. Film adds to this task the ability not merely to keep pace, but to celebrate change. It is by celebrating change that we humanize it. All the functional dynamism of changing reality is preserved and intensified by film, which is forever turning out hyped up versions of the environment which make it visible, and in some cases livable. What makes film a creative agent in change is its ability to control motion. The style of recent environmental films is a mirror of the time/space conceptual structure of today's physics. Even the interior problems of the day find solutions in the style of perceptions created by these films. Just as Freud dissolved history by revealing that the past is lived *now*, accelerated change in film brings what is to come so close to us that we can't conceive it as future. The way that this art humanizes change, creating its own space and moving time backward and forward, is by conditioning us to live more at ease amid its fluctuations.

When the young turn to films which "tell it like it is," they don't mean films which cater to the "youth revolution" (they usually fail), but those which accurately reflect a society and human life in perpetual flux. We live our lives more like Guido in *8½*—spinners of fantasies, victims of events, products of mysterious associations—than we do like *Patton* (a living historical anachronism) or Maria in *Sound of Music*, with a mysterious destiny guiding our every step. What makes *Zabriskie Point* true as experience is that we have very little more insight into the radicalization of Mark than he has, and we can hardly articulate it better than he. It would be possible, of course, for a narrator, in his omniscience, to psych out Mark for us, or for a director to structure our experience of Mark's change according to his point of view, but Antonioni has decided simply to recreate the experience. The love affair is a technological romance, in lyrical film style, between an automobile and a light plane, one confined to the unidimensional existence of surface travel with limited perspective (like the road, in *La Strada*) the other free to range freely at high speeds in three dimensions and with new perspectives. And the point made by the film is that America is not Disneyland, but Death Valley.

The new freedom of forms enables environmental films to tackle problems which cannot be treated except in these forms. Increasingly, the question asked by such films is that posed in Dennis Hopper's *Easy Rider*. Two bizarre characters cross the incredibly beautiful Southwest on custom cycles, searching for America. An alcoholic Southern lawyer, whom they pick up, raises the question, "this used to be a helluva good country—I can't under-stand what's gone wrong with it." Their shotgunned bodies lying by the side of the road reinforce the irony of the question, and of a problem posed by a new crop of American films. The notion of film as a "trip" is inherent in such films. First of all, in *Easy Rider*, the frontier journey is reversed, and the western myth along with it. The two travel through the magnificent buttes and red hills of Monument Valley, John Ford country, but they are not traveling West, to the mythical place of opportunity and freedom, but to the East. Like Joe Buck's bus ride in *Midnight Cowboy*, they reverse the pilgrimage to our past, and like him, they begin to suspect that "the Lord lives in New York City." Around the campfire at night, they turn on with pot, soaking in the ambience with long silences and cryptic, half-inarticulate remarks. *Zabriskie Point* involves a journey that comes full circle for Mark in his death, and that represents for Daria her initiation as a revolutionary. Even the peripatetic style of *Satyricon* reflects not only the ramblings of the original, but the life style of the present, a restless search for experience that never stops. In one way or another, these films become part of the class labeled by Pauline Kael the "America-the-Ugly" films. *Alice's Restaurant* has scenes of great beauty and overpowering nostalgia that make it mythic. The snowy burial of the dead junkie, with flowers, snow and a quiet poem celebrating innocence, typifies the love and peace of the life style portrayed. But the film also has the law and the draft and the contemporary paranoia that equates long hair and "difference" with anarchy. Films such as these explore the profound dilemma posed in *Easy Rider*. Freedom in life styles poses a threat to those who are not free; and if you tell these people they're not free, "then they're gonna get real busy killin' and maimin' to prove to you that they are."

However loose the structure of the environmental film, it seldom degenerates into a collage of pretty images. Rather, there is a youthful, evolving sensitivity toward what it means to be human. There is a strong humanism in these films, carrying audiences to deep levels of insight. We might say that young people are going to film for values they have looked for in vain from the social, political, or religious establishment. Modern man's morality play comes in 16mm and 35mm, but it communicates with its audience. In *Midnight Cowboy*, the reversal of the Western hero has a point (Joe Buck admits he's not much of a cowboy, but one helluva stud!). The boots, Stetson and fringed buckskin signify differently on 42nd St. than they do in the West, and it is sexual (sordid) liaisons rather than heroics which take place in fleabag hotels and subway toilets. Nevertheless, friendship is possible between Joe and Ratzo Rizzo, a man so perfectly adapted to the urban environment that he is dying of tuberculosis and other city ills. The same condemned building houses two doomed characters—the anachronism from the West and the Easterner rapidly nearing extinction. This is a world in which no one is free or proud, and in which hope means a bus ride to Miami. Love is bound to wear a disguise in such settings, and the relationship between Joe and Ratzo shows that we have to redefine manhood and heroism.

If such films have a "point" it is not a packaged view but a problem. Very little of being human happens by accident or instinct, and so we need every help to enlighten or accelerate that process. But films provide experientially a course in humanization, a sensitizing to the agonies of freedom, and a way toward emotional maturity. They allow the viewer (sensitive) to do it himself, to score a personal discovery. The filmmaker leaves his film open to such discoveries, thereby increasing its impact. Will Ben and his bride, in *The Graduate*, make it, or will they submit to suburban blight? Will Joe Buck find a new way to be a man? What will Daria do after her explosive fantasy? If there are any clues to the answers, they are embedded in the language of images, and not provided by dialogue or narration. No one tells us that Ben is alienated; we experience it in changes of focus, shots through glass and under water, where we *feel* him suffocating under his parents' aspirations. We recognize the gesture in *Easy Rider* when the profits from the heroin sale are stuffed by tube into the flag-design teardrop gas tank of the custom cycle . . . Cap'n America is screwing the country with obscene money. To see the college students in *If . . .* clearing the debris from under the stage gives us an inkling of what heritage most education gives young people. But while they burn the trash,

from Schlesinger's *Midnight Cowboy*

and set aside the old guns and bombs for use, they reverently return the medical display foetuses to the shelf . . . they know their role is to hand life on.

The spoken motive for film-going may not be "humanization," but a large part of the pleasure of environmental films does consist in the dividends of human insight. Audiences for these films tend to see more, in a film, than other audiences. They don't consider film an escape; they have television if they want to blow some time. And they couldn't care less about the threat of "corruption" from current films, simply because they are free from their elders' hang-ups. Above all, there is a desire to discuss the films seen. Everyone has an opinion on even the most difficult films, and these opinions are frequently not only independent of that of the critics, but much more perceptive. Pauline Kael performed a literary analysis on *Fellini Satyricon,* and it failed, as it must. There is no great characterization, continuity, dialogue, or narrative to the film. But those who dig it are stunned, as they were in *2001,* by the completely unique universe, the richly grotesque world that Fellini created as he released his imagination to form a world before Christianity. Similarly, to attack the weak acting and dialogue of *Zabriskie Point* would be boring to young audiences. Of course, the film lives elsewhere, in its young faces, in its lyrical landscapes, and in its revealing fantasies—love making the desert come alive, revolution destroying the model home in Phoenix.

It is said that many of the new films, the films that create an environment rather than tell a story, are products of the drug culture. Certainly the atmosphere of *Satyricon* is like an extended (bad?) trip on LSD, with human grotesqueries set against a background of lab-produced landscapes. Similarly, smoking pot is an accepted, even blasé ritual in *Easy Rider,* as "natural" as lighting up a Marlboro. But the appearance of drugs, or even the creation of druglike atmospheres is not so significant as the search for identity which both drugs and film art represent. The contemporary desire to grasp each experience, to suck it dry of substance, and to grow in the process . . . this is what lies behind the desire to "turn on." The great big beautiful spinning world that Apollo 11 showed us is going so fast that some means must be found to stop it and look at it. For some, this means drugs either to heighten the sensations or kill the pain of alienation. But for others, it may be the film experience. More minds have been expanded by film than by LSD. All art ushers man into the sublime and vicarious experience of the whole range of human emotions and choices; film does so with a characteristic totality and involvement.

The mode of involvement poses different challenges for different people. The sequence of *2001: A Space Odyssey* in which the astronaut enters the atmosphere of Jupiter has become a cultural phenomenon. For some, to sit in the front row and smoke pot is the only way to experience it. For others, the mind-blowing scenes are those in which the astronauts face "themselves" in the computer Hal, who has been programed with human emotions. There is no more forceful encounter of man with his technology in recent films, with perhaps the exception of *Blow-Up.* The lyrical treatment of violence in Peckinpah's *The Wild Bunch* is another instance. Some audiences cheer each death, and greet with applause the spurt of blood that slow motion death reveals as each bullet pierces and leaves the body. Others first savor and then gag on the surfeit of violence, reflecting on the origins of the cultural proneness to violence in the western myth that shapes the society. The topics are almost without number: the relation of media to political activism in *Medium Cool;* the killing effect of affluence on love in *Goodbye, Columbus;* the sinister sisterhood of impotency and bloodshed in *Bonnie and Clyde;* the gentle failure of flower children's fantasy of love and community in *Alice's Restaurant.* If drugs are a dangerous and ineffectual way to identify, they are nevertheless an attempt at self-knowledge for some. Films such as those cited offer a mirror in which emotional maturity, which is seldom permanent and never painless, can be achieved. But these personal values are appealing because they move a person to act from within. By making value an object of discovery, and not imposition, film makes morality indistinguishable from self-awareness.

The blend of form and content that we have described is integral to the notion of film as environment. The form must be free of literary values before it can treat problems that press on us today. Just as in the case of contemporary music, the film must work as images before it can operate as humanist values. Many of the recent folk and rock songs have lyrics which must be puzzled out before they can be identified as words . . . but the song operates on the listener long before the words are clear. There is a direct emotional appeal in the music of *Hair;* it is revolutionary aside from (or in addition to) its calculated shock advocacy of sodomy and fellatio. Simon and Garfunkel's *Bridge Over Troubled Waters,* as well as the rhythms of *O Happy Day,* are recognizable as modified gospel singing, evangelistic "uplift" songs that invite handclapping and swaying movements, whether we record and understand all their words or not. Similarly, films with genuinely humanist concerns change their audiences as much by style as by message. The overpowering nostalgia for an impossible innocence, in *Alice's Restaurant,* the bite of actuality into fiction, in *Medium Cool,* the "made in U.S.A." label on the catatonic hero of *End of the Road*—these are factors of cinematic logic, rather than the contents of a given shot, scene or sequence. We open ourselves to such films, and it is the fullness of their experience that works on us.

The films which have been cited may seem to indicate that the new audience simply goes to the film for confirmation of their own attitudes. The danger is, of course, a continuation of the old Hollywood practice of "give 'em what they want," that is, film's role as a placebo, a gentle assurance that exactly what the audience is and believes is still valid. There are enough cynical films which attempt to cash in on the "Youth Revolution" to raise fears of this eventuality. But few are taken in by such patently false perspectives as *Changes, Last Summer,* or *More.* These films are either an honest *middle-aged* person's view of what youth is about, or a dishonest appeal to youthful prejudices. *Patton* is subtitled *A Salute to a Rebel* in the hope that young viewers might think that the general was some kind of hippie in khaki. *Start the Revolution Without Me* is advertised with a giant red, white and blue screw, hoping that the title and ad will relate the fall of Louis XVI to the present. But

what the new audience of over-fourteen and under-forty wants is too important to ignore or fake. They want mind-expanding experiences they can make their own, not descriptions of someone else's trip. Relevance means, for them, using art as a way of getting involved in one's own present—in one's life—instead of being a mere spectator at the drama of self-evolution. Innovations abound, not because of built-in obsolescence, but because the world turns so fast that we need new handles to grasp, so as not to be spun off into space.

Although there may be some confirmation of perspectives in the new environmental films, they are in general more honest than the animated Norman Rockwell paintings that have been the steady Hollywood diet in the past. Moreover, such films do not merely delight, but trouble and accuse the new audience by bringing its fears into the open. Film has become a new way of escaping *into* reality. The documentary has new appeal for its ability to shut up and let reality itself speak. Shock therapy in *War Game* (a staged documentary on nuclear warfare) and *Battle of Algiers* (on wars of liberation) tends to structure the impact of apparent actuality by its sheer reliance on facts and the newsreel idiom. Actual documentaries such as *Warrendale, Titicut Follies* and *Portrait of Jason* lead us so deeply into the psyches of fellow humans that we are profoundly hard pressed to reaffirm our own humanity. The latter film, especially, is not just a voyeuristic peek at a male whore; it is a metaphor for the black man's history in America. Truth, in *A Married Couple, High School* and *Salesman* has been only partially processed—it has not yet been packaged with monosodium glutamate or other preservatives. The *cinema verité* conviction that camera and tape recorder create instant truth may be naive, but the strength of documentary remains its restoration of the role of filmmaker as discoverer.

Television has whetted the appetite for instant history, the replay of reality with the irreversibility of the past event. The Lee Harvey Oswald television murder was not the same the second time it appeared on the screen . . . it had become history. Increasingly, events are being recorded and edited for review within weeks of their occurrence. *Woodstock* tries to capture the overall impact of an event so great in magnitude that each person there could only sense a part of what was happening. As a film, its hope is to capture the myth in its making, while it still has some life. Plans for a film of the Chicago Seven Conspiracy Trial are now in the works, and it has actually been proposed that Judge Julius Hoffman take the bench for this instant replay of history. Politics as theater lacks an adequate audience without film. The result is the political film commenting on the present. New filmmakers are artistic revolutionaries, building pictures like bombs in their basements. Dennis Hopper, Aram Avakian, Lindsay Anderson, Sam Peckinpah, Robert Downey, and Arthur Penn are fanatics who believe that film can explode a sluggish society into needed change. The role is not a new one for film. Bunuel, who manifests a serene old age in his *Milky Way* (a heretic's pilgrimage through Church history), began with subversive surrealism, almost literally slitting the viewer's eye with the straight razor of his camera. His Twenties manifesto has a peculiarly contemporary ring to it:

> If only the white eyelid of the screen reflected its proper light, the Universe would go up in flames. But . . . the light of the cinema is conveniently ossified and shackled.

Perhaps some of the shackles are being lifted by the new films of today. Each director attacks some problem which we all *know* about from television, but don't really care about. After viewing the Costa-Gavras film, *Z*, the audience sat stunned at the ending when a voice from the balcony spoke for them, "It's happening here, baby!" They left in silence. *Z* is a political horror story, an ideological parable for our times. Audiences recognize in its hero (assassinated) the kind of man no longer allowed to live in our society. Anyone who has lived through the Kennedy assassinations, the death of Martin Luther King, Medgar Evers and Malcolm X, and even Martin Yablonski, will recognize the pervasive stench of fear in *Z*. Dozens of ghosts attend each performance of *Z*—the denial of demonstration permits in Chicago and Washington, the subpoenaing of journalists' notebooks, the conspiracy trials, and the

rash of bombings. The result is almost unbearable tension within the audience, especially since there is no happy ending to the film. The officers indicted for the death of political leader Lambrakis (the event on which the film is based) are now ruling Greece. Freedom's fragility under violence is a theme that will be explored over and over again in films that are made to effect changes in the audience. These changes are perhaps the greatest single source of values in the lives of many Americans.

For all that has been said of the immediacy of the environmental film experience, the audience is badly in need of enlightened education. Colleges and high schools simply do not provide the background in film necessary for opening up the riches of thought, emotion and value in the contemporary film. Where courses are available, they often become indoctrination exercises, in which filmmakers such as Fellini, Godard, Bergman, or Antonioni are accepted as uncritically as the stars were adulated in past years. Genuine film education encourages students to reflect on their film experience; without much reflection, it can be fleeting, superficial in its effect. The best response to film is to cultivate the habit of discussing each worthwhile film. Such discussions are best when they flow from our natural desire to communicate our deepest feelings. There is a real problem of an inability to verbalize the multisensory experience of an environmental film, but there must be a middle ground between a ruthless dissection of a film, and the meaningless "WOW!" which some young people bestow on their favorites. Reflecting on our experiences makes them part of ourselves, and when this is applied to the film experience, there is a carryover into other film experiences, enriching each of them. In any case, if film education in any way diminishes the freedom and delight of film viewing, it is not only superfluous, but harmful. The same might be said of critical comment on films in newspapers and journals. We don't need, any longer, the critic as arbiter of elegance who interprets his role as that of telling you to see, or not to see a given film. The critic should have the sensitivity to respond to a film, noting its failings and successes. Most criticism proceeds, as we have noted, on literary grounds, detailing the dialogue, acting, characterization,

continuity, in fact, everything but the film technique itself. The ultimate goal of criticism, in any case, is to become one's own critic, independent of any experts, secure in a personal taste with objective criteria. Criticism, after all, means taking a stand on the basis of one's own identity. To criticize poor films is not "putting down" the director for doing his own thing, especially if his thing is trite, dishonest, or so personal that it has no accessible meaning for anyone but himself.

The concept of film as an environment that one puts on, clothing himself and identifying with its rhythms and structures, is essential to the future of the art. Awareness of this factor is crucial in this age of slipping masters. Auteur theorists stand on their heads to accept the limp action of Hitchcock's *Topaz*, or Huston's *Kremlin Letter*, while fans refuse to believe that half-blind William Wyler would sign his name to *The Liberation of L. B. Jones*, a film with racist overtones. As the sun sinks on the backlot at MGM, it remains to be seen whether the new films are a late Spring or a false pregnancy. In any case, everyone interested in the new directions of cinema will have to take the young into account as the major shaping force operating in the medium. Not only the box office votes, but the actual participation of young filmmakers are changing the scene. More of the audience is approaching the film experience with some expertise of their own, while the previously disenfranchised young directors are now sought out for a low-budget success like *Easy Rider*, which will bring a return of over six million dollars for its $400,000 cost. The ingredients of the new film cannot be packaged like a cake-mix, but there is no mistaking the personal touch that permeates such films. Put together with small crews, light, mobile equipment, new techniques, by actors, filmmakers and producers who settle for very little "up front" (salary/contract) and prefer to have a piece of the action (a percentage of the film), the new cinema has a lot going for it. The feel of such a film is that it has been put together with love, bandaids, and a lot of ego. The result is not just cheaper films, but more originality, style, and freedom to tackle problems as they surface in contemporary society.

from Wadleigh's *Woodstock*

The young look in film is a revolutionary one, motivated more by a love of the medium than hatred of the Establishment. And the revolution serves notice that moviemaking is turning from profits to prophecy. The film is becoming, once more, modern man's morality play, the conscience of the age in images and sounds. The role is not a confining one, but a liberating force, freeing film for an exploration of its potential in the area of humanizing change. The prevalence of relativity in time and space will generate a hunger for moral relativity. But films such as *Easy Rider, Medium Cool,* and *Alice's Restaurant,* as well as *Putney Swope* and *End of the Road* are far from being pointless attacks or spineless spoofs. These are films that take a stand on what it means to be human. Their relativity consists in their willingness to explore problems rather than prescribe solutions. This is not to despair of solutions, but to pay the audience the greatest compliment possible—the conviction that the viewer has a heart and intellect of his own, and a free will to make his own choices. We can expect profound changes as people open themselves up, with total involvement, to the reality of the medium. If we take time to cultivate the perspective of the environmental film, we may gain an interesting window on the future, as well as a fascinating way to remain alive.

8 | KEEP THE CAMP FIRES BURNING
By Al Carmines

There are different ways of appreciating films. This is a fact of esthetic existence that audiences know more about than taste-makers. The metaphysical riches of *8 ½* or *Wild Strawberries* might produce indigestion as a steady diet. There are films we indisputably would call great but all experiences of films are not "great" and the experiences films give us do differ—and rightly so. *Lawrence of Arabia* is in no sense a profound movie, yet in its sheer visual sweep and in the excitement of its subject, it provides its own esthetic enjoyment—one which is not irreparably diminished by its lack of depth. In "camp" we have another tag to put upon the way we appreciate certain films.

Camp, of course, is not a term applying only to films but rather to a whole sensibility. The camp phenomenon was born in the corridors of English cafe society, homosexual terminology and precious esthetic understandings; it was baptized by Susan Sontag, and now has mushroomed into a tropical luxuriance in the forest of cultural enjoyment. Years before Miss Sontag dragged the coyly screaming phenomenon to the altar of public taste, camp belonged to a severely restricted and "in" sub-culture. I remember several years ago before the term was used generally, an English friend of mine described the Queen Mother Elizabeth as high camp. When I asked for an explanation I was told, "She does everything with a shade too much extravagance. It makes people laugh; and they love her for it."

Camp, as an objective phenomenon in any artistic medium then, carries the connotation of an extravagance of treatment not matched by the quality of the subject treated. But I am concerned with another aspect of camp—that is, subjective camp—or a way of appreciating things which might be called a camp reaction.

Camp as a way of reacting is a curious blend of cynicism and nostalgia. When we appreciate something in a camp way it is as if we say to our minds, "Now look, I know this isn't really good according to strict artistic judgments. But for some reason I like it and it excites me and makes me want to laugh or cry so you will just have to be suspended for a while and let me enjoy it." Camp appreciation of movies is most usually built around certain actors such as Humphrey Bogart, Mae West, Kitty Carlisle, Douglas Fairbanks, Sr., etc., but also appended to other factors—Busby Berkley musicals, 1930 melodramas, Shirley Temple movies from the early days; and soon, I have no doubt, the Betty Grable and Jack Oakie movies of the war years will join the list. Some of these movies are camp classics. When they were contemporary none of them would have been considered a classic in any sense. It is their renaissance as camp phenomena that have made them classics. Some ideas that follow this realization:

—Camp appreciation brings into play extra-esthetic considerations in our reactions. Bogart is the hero of camp not primarily because he was a brilliant actor; though he was a talented craftsman, he could not compare with Lawrence Olivier or Leslie Howard in sheer acting ability. He is a camp hero because he evokes an era of American life so clearly and so poignantly that we are profoundly, and even sometimes unwillingly, emotionally moved.

—When we tag something "camp" and then appreciate it fully we do not have to deal with those puzzling artistic questions of how something may fall short of being serious art and yet give us as much pleasure as a "classic" does. There are people who watch television with the shades down for fear neighbors will think they are low brow. Camp lets us do it respectably!

—Camp can be (not always is) a way of indulging a sentimentality in ourselves and in the artist which we would never allow otherwise. For that reason contemporary camp in legitimate theater is dangerous. It is as if a playwright, by calling his work camp, seduces us into soft-headedness through our soft-heartedness, and we end up having participated in something essentially shoddy and esthetically filmsy and false. In films it is a little different. The few self-conscious efforts at camp (that is, films deliberately made to be camp) have been such egregious box-office failures that it is not often attempted. A film usually becomes camp only through

the ripening passage of time, and by the moment it is "camp" we are able to play with it rather than have it play with us.

I think camp is far more valuable to us and our tastes however than as an esoteric movement which will go the way of all fads. It is valuable because all unwittingly it raises serious questions about appreciation and artistic quality—questions rooted in our actual enjoyment and experience. Playfulness in art is a quality we all know exists on some level, but in camp it is brought into the open. This is important as a reminder to us that on some level all art is "playful." The most profound novel, painting or drama is art precisely because it is not real life—it is "play." We have so denigrated the meaning of "play" in our society that we almost think we are insulting art by attaching this to it. Brecht, among others, understood how important it is that the audience be aware of this element of the "not actual," the "play" in art, if it is to be actually moved rather than falsely so. Only when the convention of "play" is totally accepted can what is real in a work of art really exist for us. Camp brings playfulness into open vision and thus reminds us of what is true.

Camp also reminds us that no work of art exists within a vacuum, separated from the social and political environs of its life. We have seen that American camp evokes for us an era of American consciousness. All art has this evocative quality. Great art moves subtly and deeply, beyond the obvious conventions of a time, into its structures and hidden roots. But there is no art that does not participate in its time, despite the troubling questions which this raises about the relationship of art to real life; camp reminds us of this.

Finally, in an odd way, by its very extravagance and final superficiality, camp is a refiner of taste. When we are able to identify the "camp" quality in a work or in ourselves, we learn to perceive "overdone" extravagance as opposed to brilliant style. We winnow out reactions based on cynicism and nostalgia from those based on deeper and more enduring emotions. It enables us to understand how we can enjoy movies which are even badly made or badly acted, without calling into question our excitement about serious and profound films. And the more various ways we have of appreciating movies, the more movies, strangely enough, we are able to appreciate.

A continuing camp or "semi-camp" phenomenon in the movies—one which seems destined for a surprisingly long life as camp goes—is the type of film which has come to be known as the adult western. America's devotion to the western is too well known to need documentation. From the childhood thrills occasioned by Hopalong Cassidy, The Lone Ranger, and Gene Autrey, to the great lavish sagas such as *Cimmaron,* nothing is closer to the heartbeat of the old American dream than the western. Danger, courage, the triumph of homespun justice, all were given their due in these buckskin fairy tales, and many a young boy made the psychological transfer from horses to women only with difficulty because of these romantic and stern allegories. But sophistication has now reared its painted head and producers are faced with a public that still wants westerns but doesn't want to be embarrassed by watching them. Thus was born the adult western. The adult western carries all the elements of the traditional western but the ingredients are shaken up just enough to add an element of irony or ambiguity to the old black and white ideals of the past. Not all adult westerns are camp—but most are. *Shane,* one of the fine movies in the tradition, permitted a psychological probing rare in any American film—much less a western. But such insight in moviedom is rare. *Hud,* for instance, was an attempt at a modern *Shane.* Apart from the brilliant performance of Patricia Neal it was a failure. The days of character exploration are over. The story of the lonely bad man was so overlaid with sentimentality that it no longer rang with the simple clarity that *Shane* produced.

The simple way out is camp. If the hero is also the "fool," as in *Cat Ballou,* one has the perfect camp structure. All the traditional virtues and bravadoes can be stated but with just enough of a twist to give the whole set-up a tongue-in-cheek quality. This provides the thrills but allows us to laugh at them, thus preserving our respectability.

The adult western for the most part is entertaining but trivial. Television does not even allow it the grandeur of camp. For there must be in camp at least a hint of the outrageous. And it is this quality which redeems camp from triviality. But the series of westerns televised now would not dare real outrage. The closest television program (now relegated to occasional) to genuine camp was not a western at all—it was *Batman.* But even *Batman* ended with a piddle what it began with a thud. Its brittle "pop"-oriented witticisms soon paled because the writers were more concerned with popular cleverness than grand irony. Such will probably be the fate of the adult western. Indeed, such may be the fate of camp itself. It will be swallowed up in the pop movement. This is too bad. Pop is cool and brilliant and hard-edged at its best. But camp allows us the possibility of warm nostalgia accompanied by some laughter and some tears. We need both. Camp defend yourself! The icy and slick barbarians are upon you!

9 | JEAN-LUC GODARD AND THE SENSIBILITY OF THE SIXTIES

By Heywood Gould

Every decade has its key words. Used at first as sincere expressions of the nascent sensibility of the era, they degenerate into desperate self-parody as the sensibility grows stale, and begins to crumble. A few of the key words of the sixties were "youth," "relevant," "freedom," "revolution." Alone or juxtaposed these words can be used to describe the work of Jean-Luc Godard.

Godard's career is the paradigmatic expression of the esthetic controversies of the sixties. He is the perfect example of the progression creator to journalist to politician that so many greater and lesser artists experienced during the decade. Chronologically and thematically his work adheres closely to the trends that led to the development of a totally politicized esthetic sensibility. So closely in fact that one could almost accuse him of careerism if it weren't pathetically obvious that his influence as a revolutionary cannot match his influence as a filmmaker.

As a filmmaker Godard has been enormously important. He was the first "youth" director. *Breathless*, released in 1960, was the first film to significantly separate the youth audience from the mass audience. Films as diverse as *Hard Day's Night* and *Easy Rider* can trace their ancestry back to Godard and no further.

Godard deflated the hermetically professional atmosphere that had always surrounded the making of films. The casual visual innovations of his early works created a style of low budget, limited facility shooting which has been adopted increasingly by young filmmakers.

Godard was the first director to struggle, however unsuccessfully, with the inclusion of literary and philosophical material in his work. He has tried and failed to broaden the thematic impact of the medium, but his attempts are interesting and instructive. His structure is more novelistic than filmic, consisting of chapters, not scenes, which permit him the novelist's freedom to alternate fiction, philosophy and journalism within what always emerges as a strong narrative line. He is the most erudite of directors, although his erudition at times seems pointless. He is relentlessly serious about what he does, and in his later work has given full rein to the ponderous aspect of this seriousness.

Godard brought a humorless integrity to filmmaking that had hitherto never existed. Almost every other director had been hampered by studio bosses, finicky stars and market considerations. Even the greatest auteurs have shown a profound respect for the commercial exigencies of the medium, but from the beginning Godard treated cinema as a sacred calling, more suited to the monastery than the marketplace. And because his films could reap a reasonable return on a minimal investment, he was granted total control.

Thus, with his all-consuming interest in the young, his ability to function effectively on low-budgets, his inroads into the formalistic conventions of the cinema, and his uncompromising fidelity to a very personal vision, Godard was the prototype for the generation of young filmmakers that emerged in the sixties.

Ever the restless, discontented spirit, Godard has now denounced himself and everything he did in those early days. He no longer considers cinema as an end in itself, but as a mere adjunct to the coming world revolution. He dismisses all the pantheon directors as "dead people," calls Griffith "a fascist moviemaker," and Eisenstein "the first revisionist in Russia." He has dedicated himself to the Maoist ideology with the same trappist concentration he once applied to seeing, making and writing about films. He is as stubborn an ideologue as he was a director. "A film is just images and sounds, a shadow," he has said. He now claims to be interested in "reality," and declares that "the only people making movies that correspond to real life are the Chinese."

This would seem a radical departure for the passionate cineaste of the early sixties. The man who now declares that "movies are merely a chapter in ideology," would seem to have no relation to the person who said "cinema is truth twenty-four times a second."

But an examination of Godard's career shows that his current apostasy is the logical result of a process that began with his fanatic zeal; and that his voyage from artistic to political commitment was a common occurrence in the last decade.

The sixties were a time of disillusionment. Political idols were unmasked, ideologies abandoned, institutions undermined. Artists contributed to the general disaffection by losing faith in the standards and materials of their crafts. Life had become perilous and surreal. Their fictions and artifacts seemed sinfully frivolous next to its gloomy edifice. They suffered from a sense of political impotence, and were frustrated by their inability to influence the course of events. They felt useless and outmoded, and blamed their fall from relevance on the forms that had sustained artistic creation for centuries. The "word" was repudiated in favor of the "vision," or the "shared experience"; fiction was abandoned, replaced by a kind of mendacious journalism which claimed to give a greater picture of "reality"; the plastic arts made oblique, unartistic comments on this "reality"; in the theater the audience was untheatrically "shocked" and "involved" in this "reality." Artists became commentators, evangelists. They sought to bring a greater truth to their audience than the one that could be contained in their works, thus assuming an omnipotence, which they did not have, and to which they could never realistically aspire. Continually frustrated by their lack of relevance they were driven into absurd personal and political postures. Godard, who had always been goaded by a sense of inadequacy, found it easier than most to discard all that cumbersome esthetic baggage and plunge headlong into the "struggle."

It has been easier for him because he never really considered himself an artist. He began as a journalist, and as a filmmaker was never completely able to blind his repertorial eye and turn inward into his imagination. Essentially, he was a critic floundering in an artist's medium, using his imagination to express his intellect instead of reversing the process. Aware of his displaced status he never made a pretense of creativity. "Instead of writing a critique I direct a film," he once said. "I consider myself an essayist; I do essays in the form of novels and novels in the form of essays: simply,

I film them instead of writing them. If the cinema were to disappear I'd go back to pencil and paper."[1]

One might ask why he ever abandoned pencil and paper in the first place. The answer is simple. Godard was a critic so he took what seemed to be the next logical step and began to make films. "Between writing (criticism) and shooting (films) there is a quantitative, not qualitative difference," he said.

But the distance between critic and creator is not breached by a mere change of role. Godard's pursuit of critical, rather than artistic, criteria systematically crippled his ability to make good films. In his short but prolific career, one can discern four changes of esthetic emphases, all dictated by his confusion between the critical and artistic sensibilities.

A critic's preoccupation with craft and context does not serve him well when he tries to develop a unified artistic vision. When Godard began directing, his consciousness of himself behind the camera, alone and without the powerful cinematic conception he attributed to other auteurs, made it impossible for him to work unconsciously in a style of his own. He was constantly assessing his work in terms of the styles of other directors. In the scenario for *Vivre sa Vie*, he wrote that he intended to follow his heroine not by "spying on her (Reichenbach), trapping her (Bresson), nor surprising her (Rouch), but simply following her, nothing more than to be good and just (Rosellini.)" His encyclopedic erudition fragmented his visual technique into imitations and incorporations of the styles of other directors. Raoul Coutard, Godard's favorite cameraman, reports that he would ask for a shot based on an angle seen in a Fritz Lang movie, or the left half of a shot by Jean Renoir; or perhaps a lighting set up similar to that in a D. W. Griffith masterpiece.

Godard's infatuation with the cinema was so intense that he peopled his films with characters named after movie personalities, cult auteurs in cameo appearances and parenthetical references to recondite films. The effect of all this in-joking on people who

[1] Quotations in this essay are taken from *Jean Luc-Godard, A Critical Anthology*, edited by Toby Mussman. Dutton Paperback Original. 317 pp. $2.45.

didn't understand the references was one of complete confusion. Add to this the illogical visual movement, going from rapid jump cuts to long, static monologues; and the literary, philosophical and political comments that he sprinkled through his early films and you have the essence of Godard's singularity. He was the first elitist director. From the beginning, his films were the learned conversations of a cinephile and an intellectual, meant to be shared with an audience of like persuasion. He created a global salon, which like all salons, has come to have a larger repute than actual attendance.

All of Godard's films have the virtues and defects of conversation. Their occasional moments of wit and insight are offset by long periods of boredom, repetition and uncomfortable silence. The conversationalist, no matter how brilliant, becomes a bore when he speaks to people who don't share his interests. Godard is a bore to people who don't know who Fritz Lang is, or who a character named Lubitsch should be in *A Woman Is a Woman*; and to people who cannot appreciate the significance of Samuel Fuller's appearance in *Pierrot Le Fou*, or the Bergman parodies in *Masculin Feminin* and *Weekend*. Even to the initiated, his films produce the same effect as hours of brilliant conversation. The mind reels with images and insights, some contradictory, some trivial. There is no unity of effect or experience. One has been exposed to a series of digressions and is unable to separate the wheat from the chaff.

Before he became a revolutionary Godard admitted that his best work was done when he was under the slavish influence of other directors. It seems absurd that such a devotee of the cinema should turn so decisively away from it as his work progressed. Godard claims this came as a result of his political awakening. But it could also be attributed to his inability to differentiate between the function of the artist and the critic.

The critic deals with a finished work. He has no experience, nor should he have any interest in the conditions under which it was made. He is an honest man because dishonesty, whatever value it may have in his professional life, does not exist in the critical system. What a critic claims is his opinion automatically becomes

his opinion, no matter what his motivation. The critic's sole quest is for the truth about a given work. His only obligation is to reveal this truth as simply and lucidly as possible. Rhetoric, hyperbole and subjectivism are pitfalls he must avoid. Godard, as a critic, was incisive and penetrating; he got to the heart of the matter without wasting time on an elaborate, self-aggrandizing prose style. As a filmmaker, he tried to do the same thing, but he confused the sins of the critic with the virtues of the artist.

The artist, especially the filmmaker, is a liar and a cheat, a magician with a bag of tricks and illusions that he sprinkles in his audience's eyes to mystify them or pique their emotions. He is an unscrupulous manipulator of time and circumstance; he borrows from the real world and distorts what he has borrowed beyond recognition. While Godard sat in the audience, he could respond to what he chose to call the "truth" in a film. When he got behind the camera, he discovered another sensibility in operation. "Art is the lie that makes us see the truth," Picasso has said. As a critic, but more importantly, as a man without imagination, Godard could not accept or understand this maxim.

Thus, the story of his career is one of a man becoming increasingly disenchanted with what he sees as the spuriousness of his craft, and the essential dishonesty of his performance within it.

In 1962, after he finished *Vivre sa Vie*, Godard admitted to an interviewer that he was tired and unsure of himself. "What worries me is that I'm no longer thinking in terms of cinema. . . . Now I just do things without worrying how they appear cinematically. I really don't know whether this is a good thing or not." The visual and dramatic expressions had become lies that blinded the audience to the truth and they had to be dispensed with. "I finally ended up hating the movie," he later said, "saying to myself that it is of little importance how you shoot a film as long as what you film is true. I denied the movie-loving attitude which brought me to the cinema in the first place."

Now that the cinema had disappeared for him, perhaps Godard should have returned to pencil and paper. Instead he sought a new method to justify his didacticism. He asked himself:

What to do, since I cannot make films simple and logical like Roberto's, humble and cynical like Bresson's, austere and comic like Jerry Lewis', lucid and calm like Hawks', rigorous and tender like Francois', hard and plaintive like the two Jacques', courageous and sincere like Resnais', pessimistic and American like Fuller's, romantic and Italian like Bertolucci's, Polish and despairing like Skolimowski's, communist and crazy like Mme. Dovzhenko's. Yes, what to do?

The answer was to create what amounted to a non-cinema very much a` la Godard. The conceptual cornerstone of this cinema was the construction of a dialectic between fiction and documentary. The desired synthesis was one that would impart more reality to fiction and more fiction to reality. Beginning with *Breathless*, and ending three films later with *Vivre sa Vie*, his work had been essentially narrative, and all innovations in technique were concerned with the narrative structure. If there is a concern for the documentary aspects as opposed to the dramatic, it is shown in a relaxation and expansion of visual techniques. *Breathless* and *Vivre sa Vie* are Godard's best films because they are his most cinematic. It matters little under what influences he made them; they are the work of an original mind extending the traditional concepts of filmmaking into new areas. *Breathless* is dedicated to Monograph Pictures, home of the cheaply made gangster movies of the thirties. It is Godard's transmutation of a genre he knows but has never experienced. Seeing the film again, after nine years of films, critiques and revelations, one realizes that it is Godard's artistic autobiography, his Portrait of the Critic as a Worshipful Amateur.

Belmondo (Godard) worships Seberg (American films and directors) for her easy grace and insouciance. He is a thief and a murderer (an innovator), but no matter how outrageous his actions are, they are clumsy and moral, and are leading—as he senses—to his own destruction. By contrast, Seberg is gifted with a preternatural sense of self perpetuation. As an organism she is mindless but competent, the exact opposite of the philosophical Belmondo, who knocks himself out trying to impress her and agonizes throughout the film over his inability to understand her. She has no concept of morality, acting serenely and successfully out of the exigency of the moment, a quality that hesitant, introspective Belmondo greatly admires. In the end she destroys him to save herself. She is the changeable, resourceful artist, he the suicidal, worshipful intellectual.

Vivre sa Vie was also dedicated to the "B" picture. In trying to work through this genre to a greater confrontation with preconceived reality, Godard, perhaps unwittingly, was replicating the efforts of the American "B" directors of the early fifties, who were responding to the new force of Italian neorealism. The film has the same quality of inexorable tragedy that marks the many forgotten masterpieces produced in that period, like *The Hitchhiker*, and *D.O.A.* Its slow, fragmented pace heightens the sense of imminent, unavoidable tragedy. If anything, its structure, however low-keyed and undramatic, is anti-documentary. Existential reality contains an infinity of alternatives; tragic drama offers none. From the first moment of the film where the heroine's face is presented in left profile, full face and right profile, the mug shots of an arrested prostitute, one understands perfectly that whatever follows there will not be a happy ending. The static, lifeless visual content of the first sequence introduces the atmosphere of doom that hangs over the film until its abrupt but logical ending.

It was after *Vivre sa Vie* that Godard's admitted disillusionment with the film form began. His next film, *Les Carabiniers,* seems to be almost a deliberate attempt to prove that a good film can be made in defiance of all the technical and esthetic conventions of the medium. Perhaps Godard thought that the mild, rather liberal anti-war message of the film should not be distorted by cinematic tricks he had learned to despise. In any case, the film was a failure, and he was bitterly criticized for it.

The total rejection of cinema in *Les Carabiniers* led to the second stage of his career in which the use of "reality" as a metaphor to advance and justify the narrative assumed heightened importance. In *Contempt*, the actor chosen to play an exploited artist is none other than Fritz Lang playing himself. To those who are familiar with Lang's work and the prevailing opinion that he was ill-used by Hollywood, this piece of casting had a special significance. Its indisputable reality overwhelmed the filmsy fictional constructs of the despotic producer and the disenchanted lovers mainly because it existed as a fact, while the dramatic presences had to be asserted and proved. The film which was meant to be only secondarily about the dilemma of the artist became dominated by the dilemma of Fritz Lang and the contemporary cinema.

In *Bande à Part* and *A Married Woman*, blocks of external reality (newspapers, magazines, advertisements, posters, articles of clothing) exist independent of the narrative as explanations of the characters and their motivations. In *A Married Woman*, Godard broke the words on posters and street signs into puns which commented ironically on the action. When the heroine meets her lover in a movie theater or Orly Airport, the sign "Passage Cinema" is broken into "pas sage" (unwise or indiscreet). Unwilling to resort to cinematic subterfuge, Godard appropriated huge blocks of thematic material for his "documentary" method. The "ideas" of the film are expressed in a series of newsreel type interviews with the characters giving long, detailed answers to the heroine's questions. In long monologues, shot in unvarying close-up, they tell stories and state opinions which are meaningfully related to the film, although this relevance is vague and undeveloped.

Godard's fascination with advertising and the mass media became an important thematic device in *A Married Woman*. The film is probably his most disappointing because one discerns a glimmer of interest through the miasma of long-winded monotony that prevails throughout. It is Godard, that infernal conversationalist, pausing, digressing, thinking out loud, until, just at the point when one is ready to turn away in desperation, he inserts a visual or dramatic effect that piques the interest. Disembodied hands aimlessly carressing the stark white, sexless fragments of lovers' bodies, the relentless, detached visual rendering of a quarrel, the strange tilt of the camera during a meeting at the airport, these cinematic effects epitomize the points Godard is trying to make in his tedious interviews.

Pierrot Le Fou wrote an anamalous finis to Godard's second stage. Made in 1965, it is, as critic Andrew Sarris wrote, "the kind of last film a director can make only once in his career." *Pierrot Le Fou* is a summing up of all the themes that had interested Godard up to that point. In essence, it is *Breathless* revisited; Belmondo, the fragmented intellectual, confronted by Karina, the free spirit unencumbered by doubt or morality. Only this time the intellectual does not acquiesce passively in his own destruction. He destroys Karina and then kills himself, reconsidering his elaborate suicide when it is too late to avert it. The film is memorable for its vivid, romantic color, its occasional flashes of Godardian tragi-comedy and Belmondo's energetically casual performance. Belmondo is an actor with impeccable instincts, and with Godard his instinct is always to play it for laughs. He is not, as some have suggested, Godard's on-screen alter ego, but its direct opposite. He charges Godard's lassitude with vigor and movement. He mouths his pedantic quotations with a Keatonesque solemnity that belies their seriousness. Godard's material is too formless for a performance; a mere presence in front of the camera usually suffices. He is at the mercy of actors whose strong personalities he cannot control. Thus, Brigitte Bardot and Jack Palance pout and posture through *Contempt*, Eddie Constantine looks bored in *Alphaville*, and Belmondo makes radiant comedy out of the ponderous interludes of *Pierrot Le Fou*.

Godard's work slowly developed to a point where the emphasis was wholly on a rendering of "truth" in all its absurd, illogical reality. The narrative form became nothing more than a temporal shell, surrounding agitated, disparate molecules of action. *Two or Three Things I Know About Her* is, in Godard's words, "a document, not a story," a film which "endeavors to present one or two lessons on an industrial society." At the beginning of the film, Godard's portentous whisper admonishes us to accept all things in their fictional and literal reality. We are to understand that actress Marina Vlady is playing herself as well as her character. This same breathlessly prophetic narrator whisks us through a few elementary lessons in essence and existence, warns us again not even to accept his choice of actors or locations, but to understand that they represent all of Paris and every Parisian. After a few disparaging comments on Gaullism and the artifacts of a dehumanized, urban society, we learn that the villain of the film is a large housing project on the outskirts of Paris, and the heroine, an ordinary housewife who becomes a prostitute to make ends meet. But to urban Americans, there is nothing startlingly profound about the ugliness of a housing project. And for those who admired *Vivre sa Vie*, there is nothing very instructive about a woman who becomes a prostitute because she is a metaphor for the people of Paris. Godard is not one for intricate symbolism. He states his intentions in clear, didactic tones. A publicity poster he designed for *Vivre sa Vie*, stated that the film was about a woman who sells her body but retains her soul. The trailer for *Two or Three Things* . . . said that the "Her" in the title represented "the cruelty of neo-capitalism, the region of Paris, prostitution, the bath which 70 per cent of French people don't have, the terrible law of housing estates, the physical side of love, life today, the war in Vietnam, the modern call girl, the death of modern beauty, the circulation of ideas, the Gestapo of structures." All these themes are presented in bald little vignettes with much monologizing by Mme. Vlady and constant intercuts with scenes of bulldozers and cranes lumbering over construction sites. In an effort to condemn a dehumanized society, Godard makes a film totally lacking in humanity. At the end, one wonders why he made a film at all. Why not just film the pages of Raymond Aron's "Eighteen Lessons in Industrial Society," which he quotes from frequently?

La Chinoise, which had a long, successful run in New York, is about a group of students who create a Maoist commune in a Paris apartment and spend most of their time debating tactics, testing each others' orthodoxy and refusing to relate to the exigencies of the outside world. Sitting through it is like being condemned to an eternity of attending SDS meetings. The dialectics are thick, the atmosphere soporific. The students contemplate violent action. They set out to murder a famous Russian novelist, but kill the wrong man. Less than a year after the film was released, Parisian students revolted, and Godard assumed the status of a prophet. But his attitude toward the principals in *La Chinoise* was ambivalent at best.

Weekend is a revolutionary revenge play in which a group of grim, youthful vigilantes scourge the world of its bourgeois, decadent elements. It is also Godard's first attempt at a low budget epic. Lacking the funds to hire a cast of thousands he assembled a few hundred automobiles and burned some of them down in staged accidents that occur off screen, killing and maiming a score of extras in the process. Using Godard's own reductive method one could say that *Weekend* is a series of anecdotes about traffic jams, automobile accidents, modern marriage, the youth revolution, the class struggle, cupidity, drum solos, the difficulty of playing dead in the rain with red paint on your face, and the relationship between a fetish for breaking eggs between the legs of nubile young women and the increasing sterility of bourgeois sexual relationships. Yet, its young revolutionaries are righteous, rock and roll nihilists very much in the mode of the Weathermen. No hatred that twists their young, sensitive faces, or violence that is done by their smooth, pampered hands is inconceivable in this era of insurrection. As in *La Chinoise*, Godard does a very accurate reporting job in rendering these characters, although again his attitudes toward them are not perfectly clear.

Over the years Godard's political sensibility kept pace with that of his audience. The anti-war liberalism of *Le Petit Soldat* and *Les Carabiniers,* the indignant meliorism of *Two or Three Things* . . . all reflected stages in the gradual politicization of the *avant garde.* When the decision was made that artistic expression was no longer significant to the world struggle, Godard, who had never understood the role of the artist, was only too happy to drop the pretense of being one. He now unabashedly admits to making propaganda films. *See You At Mao* is a straight documentary about the exploitation of English factory workers. *Till Victory,* financed by the Al Fatah, is about the soldiers of the Palestine Liberation Front. Godard quotes Lenin to the effect that "Art and literature are just tiny elements—a screw in the revolution." He has very happily subordinated himself to this comforting dictum. He no longer has to worry about cinematic or narrative values in his films. As long as they are about revolutionaries, and made exclusively for revolutionary audiences—two criteria which are quite easy to fulfill—they will be worthy efforts.

Sexual attitudes are not as mercurial as political ones. Godard's

treatment of sex has remained fairly consistent. Although there is very little nudity and almost no sex play, an atmosphere of sadistic menace pervades his films. Women are systematically objectified and degraded. They are bound, raped, tortured, exploited, and ignored. As prostitutes they are made to perform the most degrading acts. Romantic attachments are practically non-existent, and when they do appear are always one-sided. Only in *Breathless* do we actually see two people kissing. Otherwise, sexual contact is distant, emotionless and manipulative, following the classic pornographic pattern of exciting prurient interest while suspending moral censure. Now that Godard has joined the revolution it will be interesting to see how he purges himself of this residual bourgeois misogony.

It is fruitless to decry the steady degradation of Godard's work. Like Sartre he has made an existential decision, quite independent of intellectual considerations. As a critic he is obviously familiar with all the esthetic objections against him. As an activist he would dismiss them all as unimportant compared with the demands of the revolution.

Like many modernists Godard has come to believe that art and life exist independent of one another, and that to transcend art is to enter life. He disparages his early work because "in my first films I did things because I'd already seen them in the cinema." In spite of the fact that his best work was produced in that spirit he rejects it as unreal and dishonest. "We must turn to life again," he has written. "We must move into modern life with a virgin eye."

But an artist who loses faith in his form condemns himself to a lifetime of justifying his apostasy. His works become explanations, not demonstrations. His interest in the thing expressed is overwhelmed by his effort to invalidate the medium of expression. He produces a silent concert, a concrete poem, an eight-hour film of the Empire State Building; or as Godard has done, he degrades the form by using it as a medium of propaganda.

And ironically, the man who turns from art to politics is turning away from life to abstraction. He sees life through the monocromatic prism of ideology. Humanity is divided into symbols and stereotypes. Institutions and ideas come to mean more than people. Morality and human relationships are reduced to formulae. In spite of Godard's dedication to the cause of the downtrodden throughout the world, the only thing that is clear about his work since 1966 is that he has deliberately vitiated the film form, trampling on the standards he once held, and despaired of ever fulfilling. There is nothing inherent in his moral commitment that would prohibit him from continuing in the vein of cinematic excellence he achieved in *Breathless* and *Vivre sa Vie*. His real reasons for betraying himself will remain within him always.

10 | THE EXISTENTIAL ART OF THE NEW FILM

By Alan Casty

Everybody is talking about the movies these days, but nobody seems able to agree on *what* we're all talking about. The recent flurry of new film criticism does generally agree that the film is a director's medium (despite the still prevalent star and plot orientation of the general public) and that one can see a new work as part of a life's work that has the artistic unity of a man's personal style and a man's personal sense, or even vision, of the world. But beyond this, agreement usually dissolves—sometimes into divergent, though well defined premises, but all too often into a confusion of passions, polemics, and passing vogues.

It should, nevertheless, be possible to set forth the assumptions on which an approach to the film is based and consistently apply those assumptions in an assessment of individual films, and even in an assessment of varying assumptions. What follows is one attempt to define the basic assumptions, the common ground of the new trend in the film.

We can begin with the basic sense data of the film medium: the force, the immediacy, the tangible reality of the concrete visual image of a motion picture. No other medium evokes the sensations of reality as directly. And in a director's attitude toward this reality of the film image we have, it seems, the most valuable key to the general premises of his work.

Traditionally (and particularly as it was influenced by the American directors of the thirties and forties) the standard attitude of filmmakers was to seek the fullest surface realism possible, in the common sense of the greatest degree of imitation of real things. In this view there is posited a stable, verifiable reality—social, as it turned out in so many of the films, as well as physical. Thus, the essential job of the serious motion picture director is to use accurate and plentiful images to guarantee the verisimilitude of the neatly patterned, limited, real-life problem situation, and to keep the audi-

ence's response to the situation and characters within the fixed boundaries of an abstracted "Truth."

The most distinctive characteristic of the serious film that has developed since the emergence of the Italian Neo-Realist directors after World War II has been the change in this attitude toward the reality of the film image and thus in the use of the film image. Certainly there has been no slackening of the attempt to achieve the intense feel of a concrete reality. The change lies, rather, in a general acceptance that both the concrete film image and the visible phenomenon it represents are an incomplete suggestion, an arbitrary, if necessary reduction. The image is less fixed, contained, and categorized because the reality it tries to catch cannot be fixed, contained, and categorized. We have witnessed the emergence in the film of many of the ideas of existentialism and the methods of phenomenology that have had so pervasive an influence on all the arts in recent years.

The use of these terms goes beyond finding specific existential themes in current movies (although these, of course, do exist). For the way of seeing the world and conveying what is seen that I have been describing as the basis of the new films is a striking application of the principles of phenomenology, on which the ideas and themes of existentialism rest. The attitude of the director toward the reality of the images he creates on film is so very similar to the attitude of the phenomenologist toward the reality of the images he creates with his perceiving mind. Both believe that it is necessary (in Husserl's phrase) "to place the world in brackets," to reduce existence arbitrarily and artificially to patterns of visible and tangible phenomena if anything is going to be understood and said about it. And both presume the ambiguous, uncategorizable reality of that in existence which is beyond phenomena and thus can only be imperfectly, fleetingly grasped. This awareness of the limitations of the director's own tools has produced the dominant style of the film today.

We can examine the style in its treatment of character. The formal realism of the film image is used in various ways to convey the ambiguities of character, the elusiveness of character that the prevailing view of things holds is true (as against the clearly caused, clearly defined and limited patterns of character of the traditional realist film). Man is seen as not clearly fixed by boundaries, not precisely determinable by his properties, by an accounting of the factual content of himself as an object. And yet, it is with just such real properties, such factual content of acts, appearances, possessions, surroundings, that the film director must work.

The films of Francois Truffaut and Jean-Luc Godard define one extreme, radical limit of the new style: the subversive. The idiom that they have chosen exploits the palpable realistic feel of the film image to mock it, toys with film plot and convention—all the clichés that still *look* as real as anything else—to subvert all conventions of perception and judgment. It is an idiom that, whatever its subject, remains playful, as though play, fancy, fantasy were as important as anything else, and as real. With this idiom they play against the developing patterns of their own films—often with improvisations that result from their own associations and responses —forcing the audience to relinquish its categories about the characters and situations, to unfix its boundaries.

The style, however, is not finally subversive in the nihilistic way often ascribed to it. It is finally a fond, even toughly romantic act of protection. The elusiveness, *integrity,* energy of this self (Godard: "the complex and gratuitous illogicality of the human being") becomes the chief source of value and meaning in what is overall a meaningless situation. It subverts to keep free. This is what happens when, in a small, surface mystification, Godard, in *Breathless,* shows Michel in the back seat of a car, looking cowed and cornered, guilty—as though he had been arrested. But then he steps out of the car and pays the driver, and we have to release our conclusion about his expression. Or when, at a deeper level of mixing levels of reality, modes of perception, Truffaut, in the ending of *Shoot the Piano Player,* builds the comic gangster hunt (that has opened the film and continued on and off throughout it) to a ludicrous, parodic chase climax, only to subvert it with the horror of the gratuitous, accidental shooting of the heroine, and to contradict that thematically signficant horror with a long shot of beauty, pure, plastic, formal beauty, untainted by the *meaning* of the composition: the girl's body gracefully sliding through the snow and then coming to rest, her head lovely, couched and framed in the billowing white snow. But that image, too, is subverted by a closeup of her face—blood on her lips.

These strategies of discontinuity and ambivalence typically create in early Godard films a harder, even hard-boiled sense of a "hip" amorality, and in the later films a revolutionary callousness; whereas there is a whimsicalness in Truffaut that always seems to suggest another world that is still possible, at least in this nostalgic imagination: that world of love yearned for by the isolated, alienated boy in *Four Hundred Blows,* who, after all the blows of family and society, runs and runs through the sudden openness of nature until— blocked by the reaches of the endless sea—he realizes there is nothing he can do with that sea, nothing he can do to reach that other world. Thus, in Godard's *Breathless,* despite all the spontaneity (both of production and action within the film), despite the constant physical movement of the characters (and particularly the abruptness, the incompleteness of the actions) that serves to keep the shifting complexity of their personalities and their relationship always just beyond our classifying grasp, there is finally a kind of wise-guy ideology, a patness to the inversions. The surface appearance is always neatly false, and most importantly in terms of the characters: the good girl of the squares (intellectual, free, seeking meaning, etc.) is of course really the bitch; the bad guy, the sensual, spontaneous, free, possibly weak, but basically good guy who may get shot, but who knows how to try and live in the here and now. This ideology of "being with it," of disengaging oneself from all conventional morality and bourgeois politics, hardens even more dogmatically in Godard's *Le Petit Soldad* and more recent political films. In these, Godard's style has grown ever more adventurous in defying dramatic conventions, in insisting on the limitations of art in dealing meaningfully with reality.

In *Vivre sa Vie,* on the other hand, Godard concentrates on the elusiveness of a human being and her attempt to live her life. Except for the ending, his strategies are exceptionally appropriate and effective. The ending—in which the girl is accidentally shot in the gun battle between the pimps—seems to me to prove that the ironic use of B-picture clichés has its limits, that even gratuitousness can become pat. Godard's basic strategy is to stay outside, distant, to keep the girl as an object in just the same way she becomes only a body, an object to her pimps and clients. Yet despite the distance, we begin to sense, at the same time she begins to slowly sense the same, that she is an inside, not just an outside—is a soul. Godard first breaks the conventional reactions by dividing the film in twelve distinct Brentian sections, each with a title that summarizes its contribution. We first see only Nana's back, through a long conversation in which she breaks with her husband; later we see her back nude, being touched by the hand of a client; in the crucial conversation with her pimp-to-be, our view of her face is blocked by his head and shoulders. Throughout we stay on the surface this way only to be jarred by sudden, disconnected visual insights into her character (through brief actions and expressions) and guided by the intentionally direct philosophic statements of some of the dialogues: talking about a school girl's essay, "The hen is an animal which is composed of an inside and an outside. If one takes away the outside, there is the inside, and when one takes away the inside, there is the soul."

Rather than stay cold and distant, Truffaut maintains the elusiveness of his characters and their relationships by creating a welter of feelings, a complex mixture of modes and tones. In *Shoot the Piano Player*, he slides back and forth between the tragic and comic, the hardness of disillusion, the softness of illusion, the mockery of parody, the seriousness of realism. It is this complex of moods that helps to establish the shape and feel of the world of Charlie, the barroom piano player, as much as does the plot. For Charlie himself—who as a concert pianist unintentionally produced the suicide of his wife—cannot commit himself to any mood, any plane of his life, nor to the complex web of relationship and feeling that develops. He seeks, futilely, to escape the demands of his life, its ambiguity and fullness, only to cause it to be destroyed anew, as he, unintentionally again, destroys two people. Thus, the last sequence of the gratuitous shooting is shaped into a lingering metaphor not only of the action of the film, but of its emotional base as well, more complex than the wise-guy irony of Godard. Even its parody is meaningful. Just as the images of Charlie at the piano,

uninvolved, impassive, dangling a cigarette from his lips, are a parody of those wishfully aloof Hoagy Carmichael roles of the forties, so to be only a piano player is to be a parody of a man.

The fullness, and even the wonder, of human emotions and relationships are more directly affirmed in *Jules and Jim*, although not without some sympathetic irony on Truffaut's part.

And again the basic artistic strategy is a mixture of modes and tones: warm, Chaplinesque comedy; quiet tragedy; harsh, ironic realism; esthetic, sensual fantasy. Truffaut subverts, mocks, the romantic nostalgia of the original story and yet affirms it at the same time. He takes the basic love triangle and does whatever he can to keep it from ever fulfilling its conventional expectations. As a result these characters are kept living; beyond that they are difficult to pin down. [This is particularly true of Catherine. Her behavior shows what happens when the ideal perfection of beauty and art, of love, of a goodness (she resembles the statue found by Jules and Jim), the perfection of some kind of life force is made imperfect when it becomes human.] She is so alive, vital, gay, spontaneous, elusive; yet so trapped, unhappy, yearning, destructive. In just one of many visual examples, her last, defiant, driven, foolish, and noble destruction of herself and Jim is a lovely gag; the tiny antique car (photographed from an esthetic distance) gracefully and yet ridiculously arcing off into the water (whereas her earlier leap into the river is purely, spontaneously heroic, awesome). The sad whimsy, the parodic, deflated tragedy of the plunge of the car, of Jules' expression at the cremation, and his final walk twirling his cane, almost relieved at no longer having to cope with such raw life—all this seems an intentional reference to Chaplin, yet carried philosophically beyond the patterned Chaplin sentiment.

We can see strong traces of this New Wave style in Peter Brooks' *Moderato Cantabile* (also done with Jeanne Moreau) and even in his *Lord of the Flies* and *Marat-Sade*, and in Lindsay Anderson's *This Sporting Life*. Robert Rossen's *Lilith*, in its concern for that ambiguous line between love and power, sanity and insanity, rapture and destructiveness, clearly displays the French touch: the disjunctive cutting, the breaking up of conventional consistency of tone, of the conventional response to character and relationship. In the Peter Sellers' scenes of *Lolita,* Stanley Kubrick achieves a grotesque, perverse comedy-fantasy that is a most effective strategy for conveying Nabokov's subversion, but Kubrick doesn't carry it through the whole of the picture. In *Dr. Strangelove* he achieves more unity with the horrible disunity of subject and treatment, the intertwining of reality and unreality, of international terror and comedy; here it is more pat and propagandic, with more traditional satire simplification. John Frankenheimer's *Manchurian Candidate* has much of the same kind of perverse, macabre disunity of tone and response. In what has been called the New American Cinema there has been a strong emphasis on unrestrained spontaneity of all elements of the film, including the act of production, but—as in John Cassavetes' *Shadows*—not always with enough of a counter-balancing control, wit, craft, and taste.

Like the films of Kubrick and Frankenheimer, Pietre Germi's *Seduced and Abandoned* (and, to a lesser, slicker degree, his *Divorce, Italian Style)* maintains the complex mixture of horror and gag, evil and fun. Its humor has a strong streak of physical brutality that reminds me of the black humor of William Faulkner's South and, in the film, the hard and angry satire of Luis Bunuel, or the kind of wild social criticism found in such scenes of Jean Renoir as the last wonderful chase in *Rules of the Game.*

All too briefly, I might mention as well Kurosawa's parodic samurai's, *Yojimbo and Sanjuro,* where we encounter the same mocking of our expectations: In *Yojimbo* Toshiro Mifune's gag walk (with fine musical counterpoint) and taunting of the hired swords of the enemy, the sudden explosion into the poetry of his swordsmanship, the sudden shift to the gruesome cries and grimaces of pain, the sudden cut to the horrible gag of a dog carrying a severed arm in its mouth. In the long flashback sequences in the last half of *Ikuru,* we see Kurosawa's sense of the ambiguity of character and reality in the several different versions of what has happened, an idea and device he had earlier used in *Rashomon* (which several critics have used as a symbolic beginning of the new film).

This latter emphasis on the effects of the desires and pressures of memory is the central insight and technique of the films of Alain Resnais. Although parts of his *Last Year at Marienbad* (done with the anti-novel novelist Robbe-Grillet) result in cleverness as contrivance, more teasing than liberating, there is in the film's very artificiality its saving quality. For here we have the extremity of the photographic dilemma used to achieve meaning: whatever you photograph clearly and precisely, however stylized and artificial, seems to be real, even though no one knows which photographs are really real (although of course still just as unreal because they are in a movie). The dilemma, then, becomes a metaphor for the workings of the mind—and especially the obsessed mind—in memory: the perceiving mind that can make anything, even conflicting facts, real to itself. These dislocations of the remembering mind are given a more realistic treatment in Resnais' *Muriel.* Here the past survives again—has reality—only in the illusiveness and inaccuracy of distorting memory, but here we look at the past not only as a series of clever contrivances that become images of the riddle of the human mind in an abstract situation. Here memory is a means of discovery, of coming to terms with the present and self by characters who are believable and concrete, yet not rigidly defined. In *Muriel,* Resnais also employs much more abrupt, disjunctive cutting to effect the sense of the fragmentation of perception and understanding and to suggest as well the glancing, uncompleted relationships of the characters.

In Italy, the director that has gone the furthest in this same direction is Federico Fellini. In *8½* and *Juliet of the Spirits,* his style is the rhythmic blur of past and present, reality and fantasy, dream and wish, illusion and truth, comedy and tragedy that life is, that the self is. In *8½* it is significant that Fellini's basic metaphor for the dilemma of human perception and cognition, of human identity, is the dilemma of making movies. Anselmi, the director, after creating *8½* works of semi-art, cannot come in terms with what he has created of himself. His attempt to do so is told in a flurry of paradoxes of mode and meaning; his final recognition becomes the acceptance of this life of paradox that has been embodied in the film's style. Dead in life, Anselmi comes to a spa at which all the dead in life seek the regenerating waters of life, but futilely, clad in the shrouded whiteness of emptiness and death, descending into the white-fogged steam rooms of hell. As is typical in a Fellini film, Anselmi's plight is centered in the deadening of his ability to love. He seeks release in the perverse fantasies of a blatant mistress ("Pretend that you just wandered into this room by mistake") and of a dream girl of innocence and lost youth, also clad in white's purity-emptiness. The wife, the mistress, the dream girl in turn become characters in the film within a film; and in a screen test, other actresses are seen portraying their lives. Yet, it is finally the recognition of this complex mixture of lies and truth, evasions, creations, illusions, and memories that romantically, yet with ironic qualification, reverses the self-destructive ending and produces a happy ending, after all. The final recognition occurs beneath the grotesque caricature of film realism and of the reality of our atom world that is the "real" launching site for the climax of Anselmi's film in progress (although how this set would ever fit in with the other elements of the film in progress has its own mockery). Under this tower, the stage magician calls together all of the people of the director's creations, illusions, memories (except the dream girl whom he no longer needs) and puts them all through the dance of life, which is a circus parade, a parade of fantasy. The parade is led by Anselmi as a boy—the childhood which, in a strongly Wordsworthian sense, he can now accept as father to the man and a continuing, life-giving part of the man.

This sense of the ambiguous line between illusion and reality and, even more important, the ambiguous value of the two modes of perception can be seen in his earlier work. In *The White Sheik*, the illusions of the romantic Italian photographic comic strips are whimsically stripped to their pathetic reality: The decline of Alberto Sordi's sheik from the Valentino vision swinging mythically through the sunlight to the pudgy, sniveling captive of a motorcycle-riding shrew of a wife is wonderfully comic and touching. Yet, the film cuts the other way, too: the illusion that Sordi's young worshipper had (and lived as a kind of reality for one afternoon with him in a small sail boat) was far more alive than anything else in her life, including her new husband. Even though it has been lost, the sense of what it was may yet help her to live with the mediocrity of reality she must accept as she takes her bumbling husband's arm on the final mock-march to their tourists' audience with the Pope himself. The same contrast between the imaginary world of a continuing childhood, the necessary illusions of love, and the real world of the bleak imperfections of human relationships is central in the situation of *La Strada*—and its central metaphor of the circus—and in the emotions of its bittersweet mixture of whimsy and pathetic-tragedy. This same mood is carried on in the indomitable childish wistfulness and romanticism of the innocent prostitute in *The Nights of Cabiria*. In all three of these one feels the presence of the Chaplinesque, yet carried to a complexity of characterization and insight that goes beyond Chaplin.

In the intellectual style of Michaelangelo Antonioni, there is no place for the Chaplinesque; and yet in the recurrent characters of Monica Vitti in the trilogy there is still present the sense of innocence and spontaneous emotion surviving within the body of hardening experience. Although there is no dislocation of mode and tone, there is in Antonioni's particular form of rebellion against the plot structure of traditional realism the same result: the slow, incomplete liberation of the complexities of human character, feeling and relationship. Antonioni's form does involve the traditional careful ordering of realistic detail, but for new purposes. These details are the objects, the materials, of life that the characters live with, relate to, are in part shaped by. Through parallel or ironically contrasting emotional associations, these "objective correlatives" can suggest the emotional states of the characters, states which they themselves cannot often define or externalize; but at times these external correlatives also can take *their* emotional coloration from the projected states of the character in a subjective organizing of perception: In *L'Avventura*, what could be seen as a lovely white and modern village nestled in the beautiful hills is shaped into the embodiment of the isolation, of the deadening modernity of the characters; in *L'Eclisse*, a series of flag poles might have no particular convention of association, and yet with them Antonioni achieves the correlative of the threat of phallic, aggressive, selfish masculinity upon the girl. And further, the shape of the film itself, the carefully, lovingly composed images of the objects of life, provides another counterforce to the emptiness of the lives depicted and to the ambiguities of meaning: the counterforce of esthetic form, of beauty. These two intertwined and simultaneous uses of

the surface look of life—of phenomena, human and non-human—can be seen in the endings of the trilogy: In *L'Avventura*, the precariously tentative, hardly articulated connection of sympathy as Vitti stands and touches the shoulder of the no longer self-deluding (or at least less self-deluding) architect, collapsed before the recognition of himself, in a lingering still life of haunting beauty; in *La Notte*, the frantic, wishful and willful, attempt to resurrect the dead passion of the husband and wife, ironic against the massive and passive naturalness of the golf course—in the final long shot of their embrace, two pathetically small, squirming humans in a sand trap surrounded by the grace of the scenery and of the composition itself; and, in *L'Eclipse,* at the extreme of Antonioni's style, the long montage of objects and unrelated people, beautiful and calm in itself, yet full of the sadness of the unarticulated state of isolation, the failure of connection of the central characters who were to meet on the street corner, but do not appear.

It is helpful and interesting to compare the lingering, slow (often, to some, infuriatingly slow) sequences of Antonioni with those which were typical of silent films. They seem similar in one purpose—that of allowing the audience time to absorb things without words. But typically they are used for different effects. In the silents they served to provide a catalogue of synonyms, to build and reiterate a single, clearly classified emotion or idea. For example, in King Vidor's *The Big Parade* (which, incidentally, wears pretty well for a number of reasons) we have the long scene over the child's death bed, where shots of the child, the doctor, the other people, some hands, etc., are interspersed with shot after shot of the father's grief, shown in as many different ways and expressions as he and Vidor could imagine. On the other hand, in the best of Antonioni's work, the external objects are much more oblique in their reference to the emotions of the scene, the revelatory expressions much more ambiguous and fleeting. The general effect of the scenes is not to classify, but to embody what are still inarticulated, undefined states of consciousness.

Ermanno Olmi carries on Antonioni's methods in *Il Posto* (shown here as *The Sound of Trumpets*) and *I Fidanzati.* In subject matter, he differs in his attention to the lower, unsophisticated classes; in

sentiments, he differs in his concern for the more direct effects of modern civilization on relatively innocent, unformed emotions—the boy in *Il Posto*, the inarticulate lovers in *I Fidanzati.* Yet, Olmi reveals his characters in much the same way, as they are surrounded by the things and routines of their world, particularly the objects and petty business of their work: the crowded, yet isolating offices of the large company in *Il Posto*, the dehumanizing and isolating structures and equipment of the building site in *I Fidanzati.* In both of these films there are also parallel uses of cluttered, lonely sleeping rooms, and of the awkward alienation of people at a dance. Generally speaking, Olmi's scenes and sequences are shorter than Antonioni's, less artful for their own sake. They often end abruptly before any full climax is reached, rather than continue on through the climax to the revealing aftermaths—a typical device in Antonioni. An earlier use of this same general technique can be found in Roberto Rosselini's quite forgotten *Viagio en Italia,* in which Rossellini plays the disintegration of a sophisticated, Antonioni-like marriage against the surroundings of the poor, spontaneous, vital peasantry. Unlike the use of the surroundings in Antonioni and Olmi, Rossellini uses them to effect one of the typical spiritual regenerations in the protagonists.

A different approach to giving concrete form to the ambiguities of character is found in the mythic forms and figures of Ingmar Bergman. More than any of his contemporaries, Bergman has been concerned with broad, often abstract, existential themes. To dramatize these themes and the intangibles of subjective psychological experience, Bergman has frequently constructed paradoxical allegories. While these do vary in their particular mixture of realism, distortion and allegory, they generally tend to be less distorted than works of a more extreme expressionistic style and maintain a more consistent level of reality. That is, once you accept the premise of the situation, all the events are maintained on a consistent plane of equal reality, without some becoming more distorted, or without alternating between, say, a realistic plane and a dream plane. This alternation does occur in several of his films, such as the dreams in *Wild Strawberries,* the three distorted fantasy projections of the nurse in *Persona,* the bizarre visions and memories of *Hour of the Wolf*. Whatever the variation, he fills in the abstract allegorical roles with the realistic phenomena of human character and concrete actions. The result is the kind of parable—something like the stories of Franz Kafka—that has matter of fact contextual detail and to some degree does produce illusion, immersion, identification.

Even in an earlier, generally realistic film like *The Naked Night*, Bergman opened with a self-contained ten-minute mythic sequence that served as a parable for the torments of love in the rest of the film: in the sequence a clown's wife strays and displays herself before some soldiers at a beach, and the aging clown, pathetically yet nobly, must carry her naked body past his tormentors and up a long hill, a humanly flawed Christ bearing his cross up Calvary. In *The Seventh Seal, The Magician, The Virgin Spring* Bergman filled traditional mythic settings and forms with realistic details. Even in *The Silence*—with its symbolic hotel setting and symbolic failures of communication, its exaggerated personifications of varieties of destructive self-love and lust—the outlines are filled in, the texture made tangible and concrete with realistic details. These produce an immediate, and strong, sensory response: a woman's armpit, a breast, a buttock, a thigh, the facial expressions and the breathing patterns of orgasm or of pain or of imminent death, the positions, movements, the sounds of the act of sex (not love) in the seat of a theater, in the bed of a hotel room. In these films the symbolic materials are given a realistic texture. In his *Shame,* the opposite occurs. What begins as a relatively realistic depiction of the evils of war develops into an allegorical portrayal of the evils within man. As the dramatic emphasis shifts, so does the texture of the film. The two people who are first seen terrorized and threatened by the war—first by one side, then the other, then by partisans in between— are gradually revealed as the bearers of the personal human weaknesses and flaws that produce the public terrors. Concurrently, the scenes and shots become more abstracted, the final settings, actions, movements more directly symbolic: the wife, who has yielded to the selfish, greedy evils of the husband, shuffles dutifully after him through a desolate, rocky countryside; they await, then escape, along with others, but all separated, unconnected, uncommunicative,

on a cold, forbidding beach; as they are reduced to the essences of themselves, they drift in a small boat surrounded by the meaningless, emptiness of the cold, iron-gray water and sky, but surrounded as well by the remnants of their society, dead bodies of soldiers kept afloat with life jackets.

In one of his films, *Persona,* Bergman has explicitly dramatized his awareness of the paradox of the realistic film image—its strengths and its limitations. The film, both in technique and theme, embodies an attempt to get beyond the surface of the face (the mask, the persona, the "seeming") to the intangible reality beyond (the self, the anima, the "being"). Its bizarre opening montage (parts of which are repeated through the film)—with its cross-section of exciting stock film images, its burning of the film, its final image of a boy reaching to get beyond the giant face in the film frame—is Bergman's ironic acknowledgment of the raw materials he must use, but can imaginatively refresh and revivify.

Bergman's work is typical of the esthetics of the contemporary film. For Bergman shares with most of today's major directors this concern for depicting the reality of character that is beyond the patterns of realistic phenomena, yet can only be suggested in just these same patterns. As a result of this recognition of the limitations of realism, the new expressive style has moved toward making the intangible visual and concrete, toward capitalizing on and exploiting its own devices and techniques, rather than hiding them beneath a surface of unbroken illusion. It has recognized the limits of its own kind of perceptions and its means of embodying them. And in all of this, it has sought to find freer forms for our contemporary existential assumptions about the ambiguities of reality and the subjectivity of our attempts to know its truths.

11 | THE UNDERGROUND FILM

By Andrew Sarris

Underground films in America have come into existence largely as a reaction against certain cultural conditions. The underground filmmaker may object to the industrialization of the medium into that vague entity known pejoratively as "Hollywood." He may object to the dominant form and shape the cinema has taken not only in Hollywood but throughout the world—that form and shape being dramatic and narrative with plots and performers and a running time somewhere between one and three hours. Many so-called underground films lack story lines and actors. Many run no longer than five or ten minutes. By such standards, Walt Disney's *Mickey Mouse* and Robert Flaherty's *Nanook of the North* qualify as "underground films."

Some underground filmmakers object to the political, religious and sexual taboos imposed on the cinema. Shirley Clarke's *The Connection, The Cool World* and *Jason* seem committed to the Negro in his private hell in a way few Hollywood films ever attain. Miss Clarke's feeling is genuine and personal even if her artistic means are not particularly revolutionary. Similarly, Lionel Rogosin's *On the Bowery, Come Back Africa* and *Good Times, Wonderful Times* reflect social concerns that are considered either too extreme or too explicit for the commercial filmmaker. Stan Vanderbeek, Richard Preston and others have used animation and collage techniques in recent years to ridicule American administrations from Eisenhower to Nixon. Robert Downey (*Babo 73*) and Robert Nelson (*O Dem Watermelons*) have gone back to the Keystone Kops to ridicule such phenomena as the Presidential pushbutton and Negro stereotypes respectively. Norman Fruchter and Robert Machover have looked at Black Power, its aspirations and frustrations, in a New Jersey Community (*The Troublemakers*).

Richard Preston has summed up the feelings of the more politically oriented filmmakers in Filmmakers' Cooperative Catalogue No. 3: "I have been in the pillory for years, but now, with the aid of film, I have managed to wriggle one arm free. With this good arm I can catch and hurl back some of the garbage that has been thrown at me. And by garbage I mean the lies, the distortions, the hypocrisies that are the manipulators' weapons." The operative word in the Preston passage is "manipulators," a word that suggests a cultural conspiracy among the mass media. The ethos of underground films is anti-manipulative to the extent that experimental filmmakers both lack power and despise those who wield it. Indeed, Luis Bunuel is the classical archetype of the *avant-garde* rebel in protest against bourgeois society, particularly in the proscribed *L'Age d'Or* (1929). Jean Vigo's anarchism in *Zero de Conduite* and *L'Atalante* made of him a martyr to the French monied interests in the thirties.

In America, the impulse of resisting capitalistic control of the cinema has led to more rhetoric than cinema. Through the thirties and forties, the Left, such as it was, concentrated on infiltrating the Hollywood industrial apparatus instead of producing independent films of its own. The labor-backed *Salt of the Earth* in the early fifties was notable mainly for being so unusual an example of undisguised ideological cinema. Consequently, those who seek in American underground films a reflection of political resistance to the establishment will be grievously disappointed. The model most underground filmmakers emulate is less Luis Bunuel than Jean Cocteau, less socially oriented rebel than the self-indulgent poet.

From the beginning of underground films, a basic contradiction has confronted the would-be revolutionary artist. On the one hand, he wished to rescue the masses from their oppressors and exploiters. On the other, he was alienated from the tastes of the masses. Most people throughout the world sincerely prefer Hollywood movies to ideological ideograms masquerading as movies. Why? The optimism, the vulgarity, the escapism Hollywood represents at its worst is not too far removed from the simple-mindedness of so-called ethnic folk art. The mass of people are conservative, if not reactionary, in their tastes. This is a fact that is too well established to require further documentation here. All innovators, even the most gifted, are doomed to a period of abuse and neglect before they are accepted, if indeed they ever are accepted.

Consequently, many underground filmmakers have cushioned themselves against the shock of audience rejection by attacking the audience in their work. The cinematic equivalent of Antonin Artaud's *Theater of Cruelty* has not been articulated in print, but many underground films seem designed to punish the audience for its expectations. Cutting may be so quick, the eye strains to keep up with the changes. Camera movements may be so dizzying, and changes in focus so chaotically uncontrolled that the spectator may be compelled to turn away from the screen. Much of the eye-strain involved in watching underground movies may be attributed to a lack of economic resources for the filmmaker. At some point, however, necessity becomes a virtue as the more naive filmmaker believes it is his duty to torture his audience optically to prove that he has not been corrupted by a commercial desire to beguile it.

There is more to this attitude than meets the eye, both literally and figuratively. Classical film technique has evolved over the decades as a means of concealing itself from the audience so that the dream-like fantasies on the screen might seem real. Audiences have been conditioned to remain passive before the spectacle unreeling before them. Underground filmmakers inject irritants into their images for the sake of alerting the audience to the fact that an artist is at work. The irritants range from extreme realism (the total visual rendering of childbirth in Stan Brakhage's *Window Water Baby Moving*) to extreme artifice (the affected posturings of self-conscious transvestites in Jack Smith's *Flaming Creatures*). Few underground films allow their audiences the luxury of passivity. The artist's motivation is not so much political or social, but is rooted in his belief that the cinema, as an authentic art form, deserves the same degree of concentration that the older and more prestigious art forms attain without asking for it.

Thus, we can add to the category of underground films as social protest the category of underground films as a fine art. Here, we must make a careful distinction between those artists who seek the unique expressiveness of the cinema and those who transpose other arts to the cinema. It is not an easy distinction to make because it involves conflicting definitions of cinema itself. If an Ed Emshwiller seems to treat films as paintings in motion, it is not entirely clear that his conception of cinema leans in any way on his conception of painting. The problem is more complicated than the facile rhetoric surrounding it would indicate.

If we wish to trace the evolution of film as a fine art, we must begin in Paris after World War I with such painter-filmmakers as Hans Richter, Francis Picabia, Marces Duchamp, Man Ray, Fernand Leger, and Salvador Dali. The *avant garde* of that time has dedicated its efforts to the destruction of bourgeois values. Many of the films of that period remain in American museum archives and are frequently screened. Consequently, the experiments in surrealism, dadaism, and automatism have exerted a steady influence for almost a half century. These experiments have remained in the *avant garde* simply because the cinema always has moved toward realistic mannerisms. Paradoxically, the documentary tradition of Lumiere, Flaherty, Grierson, and Vertov has been frustrated by the fictional orientation of commercial cinema. Thus the contemporary underground in America contains both its realist factions (Leacock, Maysles, Rogosin, Clarke) and its abstractionists (Emshwiller, D'Avine, Breer, Vanderbeek). By far the largest group, however, hovers between the realistic and the abstract in that shadowy realm known as the "poetic."

The major objection to the commercial cinema is its eclecticism. Hollywood, particularly, always has understood how to cannibalize the works of foreign filmmakers. All the tricks of surrealism were swallowed up as "special effects" for purposes of trickery. Eisenstein's montage became a "time-passing" specialty of Slavko Vorkapich in Hollywood movies of the thirties. Even Eisenstein's "montage" was corrupted and degraded into a "special effect."

The underground filmmaker thus is often motivated by a messianic mission to save the medium as much as the message. Robert Kelly eulogized Stan Brakhage's *Art of Vision (Film Culture*, Summer, 1965) in terms that can best be described as messianic:

> An *art of vision* is possible in a medium which has dominated our century, and which herewith frees itself from dependence on all other art forms. Film has tended, even in the most experimental contexts, to be a composite of literary and plastic arts, dance and music, the eye at the mercy of intention, cul-

ture, pretense and imitation. Now Brakhage's *art of vision* exists utterly free of all that. It is a totality of making so intense it becomes a systematic exploration of the forms and terms of the medium itself. To explore the form without exhausting the form: a definitive making in any art is the health of the whole art, of the arts. Art in its oldest sense is skill, skill and making; the *art of vision* is the skill of making seeing. *The art of vision, The Art of the Fugue,* a presumptuous comparison only so long as we accord film only evidential value. This film makes immediate the integrity of the medium. Climax of the edited film, a new continent of the eye's sway. Mind at the mercy of the eye at last.

Unfortunately, few of the so-called professional reviewers have accepted Brakhage or his colleagues as the wave of the future. At the 1964 Venice Festival, American critics Stanley Kaufman, Dwight Macdonald and Lewis Jacobs signed a manifesto denouncing the New American Cinema as an artistic movement. Most underground films are never even seen by the regular reviewers, and few of those seen are treated with the slightest respect. Nor has a mass audience materialized for these works. What has happened, however, is that the underground has found a persuasive mystique through the extraordinary efforts of Jonas Mekas, editor of *Film Culture* magazine and columnist for the influential *village voice*. Mekas, more than any other individual, has grouped together the great majority of dissident filmmakers into a well organized underground movement.

Mekas has devised an effective strategy to publicize the underground movement. Instead of apologizing for the more outrageous works, he proclaims their sublimity. Some unfriendly observers have likened Mekas to Marshal Foch in charging when he is most beleaguered. Most of the controversies surrounding Mekas in recent years have concerned two filmmakers, Jack Smith and Andy Warhol. Jack Smith's 60-minute 16 millimeter *Flaming Creatures* received *Film Culture*'s Fifth Independent Film Award back in 1963. Previous *Film Culture* Awards had not created much stir. John Cassavetes' *Shadows* (1959) had been respected generally as an attempt at improvisational realism on the New York scene with a matter-of-fact treatment of racial traumas. Robert Frank and Albert Leslie collaborated on *Pull My Daisy* (1960), a chronicle of the Beat Poets, Allen Ginsberg, Gregory Corso, and Peter Orlovsky, to the narration of Beat Novelist Jack Kerouac. Frank was a distinguished still photographer, and Leslie a respected independent filmmaker. For that matter, Cassavetes had been a relatively successful actor in Hollywood before *Shadows* and had demonstrated his directorial abilities further with *Faces and Husbands*. Ricky Leacock and the Maysles brothers were honored in 1961 for their vivid documentary of the late John F. Kennedy during his Wisconsin primary battle against Hubert Humphrey. Again, Leacock and the brothers Maysles were eminently respectable by the most rigorous professional standards. The award to Stan Brakhage for *The Dead* and *Prelude* in 1962 was somewhat more controversial than its predecessors, but no great furor was created. Then came 1963, Jack Smith and *Flaming Creatures,* police persecution, charges of immorality, and enormous publicity for the movement. Mekas described *Flaming Creatures* in terms that were defiantly superlative:

In *Flaming Creatures* Smith has graced the anarchic liberation of new American cinema with graphic and rhythmic power worthy of the best of formal cinema. He has attained for the first time in motion pictures a high level of art which is absolutely lacking in decorum; and a treatment of sex which makes us aware of the restraints of all previous filmmakers. He has shown more clearly than before how the poet's license includes all things, not only of spirit, but also of flesh; not only of dreams and of symbol, but also of solid reality. In no other art but the movies could this have so fully been done; and their capacity was realized by Smith. He has borne us a terrible beauty in *Flaming Creatures,* at a time when terror and beauty are growing more and more apart, indeed are more and more denied. He has shocked us with the sting of mortal beauty. He has struck us with not the mere pity or curiosity of the perverse, but the glory, the pageantry of Transylvestia and the magic of Fairyland. He has lit up a part of life, although it is a part which most men scorn. No higher praise can be given an artist than this, that he has expressed a fresh vision of life. We cannot wish more for Jack Smith than this: that he continues to expand that vision, and make it visible to us in flickering light and shadow, and in flame.

Flaming Creatures is the description of an orgy involving homosexuals and transvestites, but the action is curiously lethargic. The characters are content to pose passively as they re-enact their wildest fantasies of old Hollywood movies. Jack Smith himself has written eloquently about his passion for Maria Montez back in the forties. Certainly, Smith fulfilled the historic function of the *avant garde* in shocking the bourgeoisie, but he had drifted a long way from Antonin Artaud and Luis Bunuel. What is most shocking about Smith is the limpness of his gesture. He shocks simply by not caring whether he shocks or not. He describes a world that exists apart from ethics and politics, and yet it is a world that is real in its very artifice. It is as if Jack Smith were depicting a race of mutants that had been spawned by the dream-like apparatus of the Hollywood spectacles. But what really irritated many worthwhile supporters of the *avant garde* was Smith's apparent amateurism. Cheap, second-hand film stock and inferior equipment produced a crude, eyestraining effect that seemed to insult even an *avant garde* audience.

Nevertheless, Mekas stuck to his guns, and there was something admirable in his defense of a filmmaker who was nothing more than a filmmaker. At about the time *Flaming Creatures* was released in New York, Jean Genet's long suppressed *Chant d' Amour* came into the country. Those who complained of the homosexuality in *Flaming Creatures* were strangely respectful toward Genet's more flagrantly erotic treatment of the subject. Genet's literary reputation conferred cultural authority on his film, whereas Jack Smith's pictorial talent was overlooked.

Flaming Creatures was a turning point in the American underground, not because of any stylistic breakthrough, but because it represented a new principle in the promotion. Mekas began to appeal to film poets everywhere to make their own movies. The 16-millimeter mystique of the fifties was reduced to the 8-millimeter mystique of the sixties. The notion of "home movies" was glorified into personal poetry. The filmmaking establishment with its financiers, its big stars, its fantasy spectacles, its closed unions, its shameful compromises was completely bypassed. Mekas' message was beamed especially at the college students of America. "Forget Hollywood," they were urged. Get your own cameras and film and make your own movies. This message has irritated many film educators who consider Mekas a demagogue and a charlatan. Professional critics consider Mekas a positive menace to their well-ordered existence and the comfortable relationship they enjoy with the film industry. What everyone has failed to realize is that cinema is becoming the most fashionable means of expression, and with or without Mekas a revolution of tastes is in the offing.

Mekas himself is something of a mystery. There is in him both the political activist and the quiescent mystic. His own films (*Guns in the Trees* and *The Brig*) are deeply committed against the American Way of Life. Yet many of the artists he has encouraged are relatively apolitical. The most interesting of these is Andy Warhol, the high priest of Pop Art in America. Warhol is maddeningly ambiguous about his own role in the underground movement. *The Chelsea Girls,* one of his most successful films and the first to be received "above ground" can best be described as anti-cinema. Warhol simply plants his camera in a fixed position and lets actors perform in front of it. Unlike Jack Smith, Warhol is never too shocking in a visual manner. Warhol has been a successful pop artist although some art critics have questioned whether he is an artist at all. He functions as a passive receptacle of experience. He accepts his environment totally. He accepts his history totally. He expresses no desire to shock, to outrage, to reform, and yet he arouses violent emotions in his audience. His films seem to affront the artistic process itself with their lazy, indifferent technique, their lack of editing or even satisfactory splicing. Warhol professes to love Hollywood movies precisely because they are superficially attractive and shallow. His utterances mark him as an anti-intellectual, and his subject matter as something of a frivolous dandy, and yet he, too, represents a turning point in the *avant garde*. Behind his mask of passivity, Warhol represents a generation not in revolt, but in withdrawal. By accepting all the gaudy consumer goods of capitalism, Warhol makes Americans confront their new idols. (Warhol's most successful artifact was a literally reproduced Campbell's Soup can.)

However, Mekas' defense of the assorted outrages perpetrated by Jack Smith and Andy Warhol has almost obscured an interesting development on the surface of American society. America, and particularly New York, had witnessed the final death throes of puritanical censorship. Only a few years ago, films available in Paris were banned in New York. This development offers the *avant garde* both a challenge and an opportunity. No longer will the underground be able to justify its existence solely because it wishes to shatter certain taboos. Nor will the social virtues of its political gestures exempt it from critical judgment. American filmmakers have more freedom and opportunity today than ever before. There are more than 800 film courses being given in colleges across the country. Yet, there are serious obstacles to a renaissance in the cinema.

First and foremost is the sense of alienation that persists in the sensibilities of the underground filmmakers. Shut off from the large audiences that attend the commercial cinema, they have also shut themselves off from the larger themes and more challenging characterizations. A small coterie of critics and enthusiasts is turning out an ever-expanding literature on the movement, but the films in question are not calling into question traditional values, but rather celebrating the glorious solitude of the narcissistic artist.

There is a strong possibility that the *avant garde* will be swallowed up by the revolution in cinema it helped set into motion. From the very beginning, the cinema was a spectacle for the masses, an art form for the socially oriented artist. The introverted poets have always subsisted, if at all, at the edges of the medium. The delicate fantasies of the late Ron Rice, the elegant frames and fancies of Gregory Markopoulos, the impish scrawls of Carmen D'Avino, the anarchic animation of Harry Smith all seem destined to languish in the limbo of museum exhibits. The filmmaker of the future will seek to surmount the limiting doctrines of Beat and Pop Art as Bunuel and Clair once surmounted the limitations of Dadaism and Surrealism.

The important thing to remember is that underground films in America are still in a state of becoming. The experiments continue. The cameras proliferate, and a continent is rediscovered. For the first time in history, there is a generation of young people aware of the potentialities of the camera as a means of poetic expression. As Jean-Luc Godard observed, ''We are the first children of D. W. Griffith and Sergei Eisenstein.''

Nonetheless, young American filmmakers have not been hypnotized by the claims of the *avant garde*. Young filmmakers seem to show a preference for the more fashionable European directors—Antonioni, Fellini, Bergman, Godard, Truffaut, and Bunuel—even Richard Lester who directed The Beatles in *A Hard Day's Night*. If there has been one underground film that has attracted attention throughout the country, it has been Kenneth Anger's *Scorpio Rising* with its sacrilegious treatment of a motorcycle cult worshipping such disparate deities as Marlon Brando, James Dean, Jesus Christ, and Adolf Hitler.

The one American director most young people admire is Stanley Kubrick, particularly since *Dr. Strangelove* convulsed American audiences in 1964 with its darkly humorous satire of the Bomb as the end-all of human existence. In a sense, Kubrick came up from the *avant garde*. His first films—*Fear and Desire* and *Killer's Kiss*—were frankly experimental films financed by Kubrick's relatives. He succeeded in obtaining a Hollywood contract, and the rest is conventional film history.

Kubrick used the underground only as a means of surfacing to a more popular cinema. Most young filmmakers would prefer to follow Kubrick's path than Anger's or Warhol's. This is the final victory of capitalism in the cinema. The poet surrenders to the producer. The socialist filmmaker will prefer to follow Kubrick's path as much as the capitalist filmmaker if only to influence a larger audience. The temptation of the mass audience is a problem film art has faced everywhere from the very beginning of the cinema.

12 | FILM CRITICISM AS PROCESS

By Roger Ortmayer

The search for esthetic keys that will unlock the mysteries of art persists. Somehow, sometime, people seem to believe, the formula will arrive which will clarify the secret, penetrate the impenetrable. Hopefully, this revelation will be verbal. The meaning will be grasped according to a verbalized system. The knowing subject will again have conquered by stuffing the elusive object into his bag. The hunt will be over; at least until the foxy artists show up with new tricks. Then set the pack loose again to box in the quarry.

The trouble with this description is that it is a stupid analogy. It rests on assumptions that may have some cogency "back there" (even this claim is dubious), but for the last part of the 20th century are misleading. Intellectualized systems and doctrines in art are not only suspect, they are mischievous. They have been used, mostly, to explain rather than realize. The result has been further to alienate the artist from the company of those who patronize, use and experience art. They have been made dependent upon the critic's insight rather than their own experience and participation.

It is nearly one hundred years, now, since Nietzsche demolished theories of categories. It is odd that so much criticism never got the message. Criticism has persisted in separations and categories. It claimed to give clues and channels to the "understanding" of art. Romantic and classic, subjective and objective, personal and impersonal, intrinsic and extrinsic, and on and on . . . All the while the arts were going their many ways. Any convergence with the criticism has been largely coincidental.

Film and the other arts

Films, of course, have not developed in an arts and social vacuum. They are a part of a context, and it is useful to see films as part of an evolving pattern. Painting, drama, sculpture, poetry, and novel have many and varied relationships and contributions to cinema art. Comic strips and other multiple media are closely associated.

One can make a plausible case for a step by step evolution of films from antecedent arts, just as, for example, some art historians have "explained" the Gothic cathedral by assembling the vision and engineering of Romanesque art and architecture.

The Gothic cathedral, however, was as much a mutation as an evolution. It was unique. It could only have happened through the vision of men such as Suger of St. Denis, the technical virtuosity of the 13th century artisans and the building stone of France, and other factors peculiar to the time such as an ascendent French monarchy. It was related to its past, but such facts do not suffice to explain the Gothic.

Film is also decisively singular. It could have happened in no other time. It is the peculiar art of the 20th century. It is a mutation, impossible without such men as Edison and Griffith, the technology of the electric age, the communications needs and sensitivities of this century.

The singular aspects of film art should be assessed in relation to the other arts of this time. In 1914, by the beginning of World War I, it was clear (at least it is clear in hindsight) that something radical had happened which was altering the vision of the artists. In painting, the *Fauves* had held their infuriating exhibitions. These artists, headed by Matisse, had flung "a pot of paint . . . in the face of the public," according to critic Mauclair. The movement became known as that of the wild beasts *(fauves)*, after an epithet of Vauxcelles who also coined the term "cubism." Delighting in the free use of color, inconsiderate of representation of something outside the painting itself, the artists associated with the movement developed their own manners of self expression, with a continuing influence among the German expressionists and other modern movements. In France, Cubism soon distracted most of the artists by its fascination with masses, volumes and planes. The *Fauves* took their cues from Gaugin. The Cubists looked back to Cézanne. But, whatever the direction, they had so radically altered the visual image as to make the venerable cliches as to what art is and how it is to be seen no longer relevant.

Nor were they movements in any doctrinal or ideological sense. The participants were impassioned and there was high tension, but no formal regularities. Cubism did have a kind of coherence and progression that the explosive character of fauvism could not tolerate. Together they shifted the base and the process of visual perception for our time.

By 1914 similar shifts had occurred in most of the other arts: Joyce had finished *Portrait of the Artist as a Young Man* and was at work on *Ulysses,* and the contour of the novel took a radically different shape; Isadora Duncan was shattering the classical tidiness of dance; Stravinsky had already escaped through a back window at the Paris Opera at the premier of *Rite of Spring;* the mysterious beauty of pure form in space was taking shape as Brancusi's "Bird in Space" was sculpted; Sullivan had built the prototype of the skyscraper; Cummings and Eliot were already published poets and Rilke's *Duino Elegies* were half written. And Griffith, Sennett, Ince, Zukor, Lasky made Hollywood. DeMille and Apfel had finished *The Squaw Man.*

The most laggard of the arts was drama. Yet its critical conventions were those that came to be applied most vigorously, and disastrously, to films. Both the ancient prescriptions of dramatic unity and the notion that it all was essentially literature and therefore must adjust to essentially literary meanings were the accepted criteria of analysis and criticism. The newest of the arts fell into the critical catchall of the most persistently foot-dragging, backward-looking of the critical pockets. The singularity of films, their uniquely cinematic form was largely unobserved, while largely irrelevant dramatic literature tests were applied. The irony of the situation was that what was primarily visual was criticized in non-visual terms.

Yet motion pictures were providing precisely the technique and momentum that painters from Klee to Rauschenberg, the Dadaists, Surrealists, Futurists, and others in the *avant garde* of the visual arts were endlessly seeking, *i.e.,* a continuity of process in place of *stasis.*

Running throughout the first two generations of this century, the interplay between the artists who create art "objects" and those who deal primarily in experience is a fascinating account of the disintegration of an historic order and the maturation of a novel form. One of the most off-beat movements, Dada, was of seminal influence:

> "...Get ready for the action of the geyser of our blood
> —submarine formation of transchromatic aero-
> planes, cellular metals numbered in
> the flight of images
>
> above the rules of the
> and its control
>
> BEAUTIFUL:"
> (—Tristan Tzara: *Seven Dada Manifestoes,*
>   from No. 3 "Proclamation without Pretension.")

While the Dadaists professed a new stance of nihilism in their attacks upon fine arts and the conventions of morality, religion, logic, and probity in general, what they actually did was to help in the creation of a new esthetic, a freedom of imaginative production that would be discontinuous from the classic claims. The eruption they stimulated provided a new continuity of free form, of process unchained from the hypotheses and assertions which had undergirded art for 2,500 years.

It was inevitable that some of the Dadaists and their successors, the Surrealists, were drawn to the possibilities of the fledgling film art. Film was lowbrow and unpretentious, scorned as having nothing to do with art, vulgar and humorous. But best of all, film violated all the rules. It had freed the image to move. The results could be hilarious and sentimental, bizarre and realistic, all possibilities that delighted such artists.

Marcel Duchamp's *Nude Descending the Stair,* the scandal of the 1913 New York Armory Show, was a kind of cubist-futurist painting that preceded strobe flash effects in still photography. It attempted movement in easel painting. After a few more years of painting activity Duchamp quit painting, apparently feeling there was no place left to go. In the meantime he had diverted sculpture from its preconceptions with his "ready mades": snow shovels, bottle racks, bicycle wheels, urinals, etc., which he insisted upon placing in art exhibitions to face the furious rejections of the curators.

In the meantime, the most perceptive of the artists of the first half of this century, Paul Klee, worked at an art of seeing that was process. Movement, he insisted, was the essence of painting. He felt that everything moved—the painting itself, the eyelids of the artist, the eyes of the viewer. He listed the formal elements of drawing as points, lines, space, energy.

When, following World War II, the center of the art world shifted from Paris to New York City, it was the action painters who provided the impetus: Pollock, de Kooning, Klein, and their colleagues made the act of painting the work of art. Without preconception they attacked blank canvasses, boards, walls. Their work had tremendous emotional intensity; it vibrated with a mysterious fervor and shock. Their paintings could not be framed; they seemed always to be in an act of becoming, unfinished, moving.

Even the momentum of action painting was too formal for the pop and kinetic artists of the late '50's and '60's. They gave birth to happenings, and in turn happenings gave shape to their art. It was derisive, dramatic, ironic and often ephemeral. When Yves Tinguley's sculpture, after an exhibition period in the garden of the Museum of Modern Art, proceeded to self-destruct, it demonstrated how far the disintegrations of the art "object" had gone. The emphasis had shifted to the art experience.

The moving picture

Movies, as we know them, could have happened only in our time. Although there were many experiments and toys that made pictures move and utilized the "persistence of vision" principle, it was not until a strobe safe form of light and an efficient powered mechanism to move a flexible film became available that the art could be satisfactorily realized.

The self-conscious fine arts world was quite oblivious to the novel art, which had been designed by an assortment of tinkerers and developed by a batch of quixotic, often nearly illiterate, entrepreneurs, most of whom felt that "art" was for the birds. They knew, however, what was fun and would make money. They were not locked up in quests to resolve the problem of movement nor the quintessence of time. But they had an enthusiastic intensity for the job of making quick motion pictures; keeping a jump or two ahead of creditors, patent infringement suits, plot stealing and having a good time in the process. They were improvisers extraordinary, making use of any crowd, event, or crisis that showed up and turning it into a story line later. They showed actors into and out of all possible street scenes, grinding out one and two reelers and only gradually working their way into the longer films. The expectancy of something really important was present. When Griffith's *The Clansman* (later *The Birth of a Nation*) had its first showing in Los Angeles, the audience was made up mostly of people who were involved with films. The reaction to the showing was one of wild ecstacy. They literally tore the show place apart. Something new had been created, a fulfillment and a portent.

It had come out of the quickies, but was itself, as the crowd intuitively knew, a mutation, something different and new and of seminal import. It was the motion picture, an art form that was to become the primary locus of identity and meaning for the 20th century.

Finally, the image had been unfrozen from its ancient *stasis*. It moved in actuality, not by inference. Baroque art of the 17th century, for instance, explored many of the possibilities of implied movement. The canvasses of Rubens were often huge, filled with swirling figures, interpreting heroic events and persons. But it was all frozen, an illusion of motion and would never go on and be completed. The marvelous baroque churches of the period were built to image a vortex of movement. Their naves and sanctuaries radiated triumphant encounter of the heavens and the earth; but in the end their figures were frozen plaster and their panoramas a vortex implied. Actually they were frescoes and murals, materially little different from similar works of the Greeks and Romans.

Movies were a release from that ancient frustration of the artist thawing out, the frozen image, the possibility of art that moved in actuality.

The moving picture changed the style of the artist and his relations to his public. The filmmaker was seldom the solitary studio artist, working in isolation. He was a group: writers and researchers, camera and light and, after 1929, sound men, property men, script girls, directors, actors and actresses, editors and producers. A Robert Flaherty, frozen in with his Eskimo friends, shooting thousands of feet of film, later emerging and editing his treasure into *Nanook of the North* was the exception.

The underground filmmakers of the '50's and '60's came the closest to the romantic artist style, working out of lofts and basements, scrounging for film and cameras, producing brief, usually erratic pieces with truckloads of banal results in which were hidden some marvelous gems, revealing the mysterious possibilities of filmic art which the huge commercialized productions could never touch. But even these loners organized themselves into cooperatives to make available the equipment necessary for shooting and processing and locating some channels for distribution and exhibition of their work.

For the public of films was also a radical revision of what an art public had always been thought to be. The painter and sculptor were tied to the patron, usually a person of wealth or public influence. The general populace might benefit through exhibitions in churches, official buildings, or, in the modern age, museums. For films, however, it was the general public that counted. Ways had to be located to make the common people sit down and see. It was the mass audience that counted, not the exceptional patron.

The obliviousness of the arts community to film in the first half century of its development is to be accounted for by the snobbishness and preconceptions of the patron circles. They looked upon art as a possession and were jealous of its scarcity value. Even the era of printing had made little impression, the graphic arts being considered minor at best. In contrast, films were popular arts, having something to do with media and mass communication but hardly worth serious consideration by the art snobs. Only slowly has the old arts community become willing even to admit films among its accessions, and even today the majority of art museums look upon films as a kind of minor adjunct to essential affairs. A museum, or individual, cannot own a film in quite the way they possess a painting, cutting off the essential distinction of the art snob.

Interestingly enough, one of the cutting edges of the more private arts in late years is what some call conceptual or systems art. It abjures the art object and its possession. It may deal with data and records, but the work of art is an event, or an experience, an increment from an investment or a loss, as in giving blood to the Red Cross. It is bringing the gallery and museum interests close to that arena which has been explored for a long time by films.

The technological factor

As we have come to realize something of the nature of process in art, we have been forced into an accounting of the physical apparatus, both in the "production" (creation) and the "consuming" (appreciation) ends of the program. When art criticism had only to deal with the art object, it developed logically coherent and simplistic analyses. They were immensely persuasive because they seemed to hold together so plausibly. They were as the closed systems of Newtonian physics or the scientism of early sociology.

For the sophisticated scientist, however, the old hoped-for objective reality of particles "out there" has turned out to be too rough a simplification. As Heisenberg says: "When we wish to picture to ourselves the nature of the existence of the elementary particles, we may no longer ignore the physical processes by which we obtain information about them. . . . it turns out that we can no longer talk of the behavior of the particle apart from the process of observation. . . . We can only talk about the processes that occur when, through the interaction of the particle with some other physical system such as a measuring instrument, the behavior of the particle is to be disclosed." (Werner Heisenberg, "The Representation of Nature in Contemporary Physics" in Rollo May, ed., *Symbolism in Religion and Literature*, George Braziller, 1960, p. 220.)

Film criticism, which has looked upon an 80-minute sequence upon the screen as the subject to be evaluated according to preconceived system of rationalization, has been as misleading as simplistic scientism was for physics and chemistry. As with the scientist exploring the physical universe, through his instruments, whether electronic or mechanical, we only see what is on the screen through the gadgetry of filming and projection, and the continuity of a film moving at 24 frames per second. (The unsophisticated film viewer often gets a distorted notion of what many early films were really

like because of having them projected at the standard 24 frame per second speed. The hopped up speed that seems so hilarious is the result of overspeed. For example, *The Birth of a Nation* was shot at 12 to 18 frames a second. Reviewing it at the 24 speed is a distortion. Also, especially with many of the old quickies, the cameramen often found themselves running short of film before they had finished a sequence. They simply slowed down the film take, but when projected at a constant speed results in some seemingly furious activity.

Deliberate contraction of time can do marvelous things in showing how a flower blossoms or a horse runs. Seventy-five years ago the demolition of the Star Theater was projected in a 30 second period, a result of a take at the rate of one frame per 30 minutes. Oppositely, slowing of time is achieved by speeding up the camera and slowing down the projection.)

The realization of space is similarly rearranged, distorted, and amplified in films. Huge screens, wrap-around projections as in Cinerama, magnification of certain features by close-up and then projection on huge screens, give a sense of proportion and scale impossible to direct sensory experience. It makes visible a metaphorical impact that literature has been able only to suggest.

In film, the projected image is a part of a process, a kind of dialogue as well as a record of what has taken place and is being shown. Film criticism should work more at dealing with this transaction. We know, gain information and data, make judgments by taking into account the technology of the process. The technology interprets the contours of visibility—the shape, color and placing of images as it shrinks or expands time. This interaction of mechanics and image is also mixed into the participatory process of the film viewer. Film criticism today tends to fail totally, when it is unaware of the interaction of the image with the physical system producing it.

The viewer as screen

In 1968, I met with the committee which was to make nominations for the awards by the National Council of Churches for the outstanding films of the previous year. There were some excellent films to consider: *The Graduate, In Cold Blood, Petulia*. I kept trying to insert Warhol's *Chelsea Girls* for serious consideration. The committee reacted with non-belief or derision. I could not be serious, could I? Support for my award candidate was nonexistent.

The committee members reflected the critical consensus of *Chelsea Girls* at that time. (Since, however, noting that people insisted upon seeing the film, that it was being paid attention in serious circles, some persons have done a bit of reassessment. In 1970, the Museum of Modern Art in New York City included *Chelsea Girls* as one of the ten pacesetters in its review of the decade of the '60's.) If they even bothered to look at it, most critics considered it an interminable bore. They were only grateful that its original eight hours show time had been halved by Warhol's decision to cut the film in half and show both parts simultaneously on a split screen. And such a trick just showed the lack of seriousness of Warhol as an artist. He should have, the critics reasoned, carefully edited the film to an appropriate length. Contrasted to an Antonioni, who, if he was not quite certain about the color of the park grass in *Blow-Up*, would have it painted the exact shade of green he needed, Warhol was lazy and amateurish. They pointed to the sloppy camera work, faulty sound, inept lighting, and asinine dialogue as evidences that they could not take any such work seriously. It was a preposterous joke to offer the pretense of serious filmmaking.

The fascination about this typical brush-off of Warhol's film is that it is correct in each of its points and ridiculous as a conclusion. I was serious in proposing *Chelsea Girls* for the award because Warhol had made something which was essentially filmic. When I saw it at its original showing in New York, late at night, I was so bored I, too, went sound asleep and finally left before seeing it all the way through. I found its subject matter silly, occasionally offensive to my taste, and I would have been rather hard put to find much redeeming social value in it. The odoriferous cellar off 41st Street where it was shown was about as odd a contrast to an old Balaban and Katz movie palace as one could possibly locate. I never did quite figure out whether the recurring out-of-focus of one or both of the frames was the result of the original camera work or indifferent projection. The camera work was static, although Warhol certainly did seem to like his new zoom lens. The lighting was irregular, usually on the poor side. The characters were often self-conscious . . . . on and on with the negatives.

Which demonstrates how beside the point such criticism is. *Chelsea Girls* exists as an important film.

In *Last Year at Marienbad*, Resnais forced the audience into participation by making its members tell the story. The film posed the questions, visually, and left the resolution, the meanings, to those who watched the projection. At Expo '67, the Czech film theater invited the members of the audiences to vote their opinions and a tabulation of the votes decided on what ending the film would take. These and other such experiments have been useful in making people at the films aware of themselves as participants.

Warhol has gone a step further. He made the patron a screen, not by projecting images on him, but by bouncing the image continuity off him. The viewer has no refuge from the film by recourse to tangential criticism or analysis. That is, there is no plot; the story continuity is mixed-up or irrelevant. There is no delight in the technical virtuosity, as with Resnais, who is one of my favorite filmmakers, one in whom I delight much more than I ever will in Warhol. All that we have is film. Warhol gives nothing but film. And just now that is giving everything. The intellect is barely touched, but neither are the emotions. The cost of making the film was puny— perhaps $3,000 to $4,000. The actors were friends of Warhol, and Warhol, as usual, was in a do-it-yourself mood, making some two or three full-length films a week at the time.

Process criticism

Process criticism deals with films as such. The focus does not repudiate ethics, sociology, psychology as valid humanistic studies, but realizes that as disciplines they are inadequate for film analysis. It deals with the art of the film rather than seeing it as exemplary messages (or the opposite in graduations between the exemplary and the obscene). At the same time, such criticism realizes that the film is public, that it is human beings who are involved with all their delights and hang-ups, predispositions and anticipations, prejudices and dreams.

Process criticism must be contextual, but the context is one geared to films rather than ideologies. The context of criticism is filmic. The good and the bad of evaluation is made in consideration of the cinematic process rather than imposed from other arenas.

The awards given annually by the National Council of Churches, referred to above, recently have been related to those given by the National Catholic Film Office. For some years, these Protestant and Catholic groups made awards to films that primarily satisfied institutional religious demands. That is, they thought of religion in purely extrinsic aspects: the story lines would deal with biblical narratives, or clergy, or church mission projects. The award winners had to satisfy specific moral prescriptions. The fact that they were dealing with films and not with church propaganda did not seem to enter the consciousness of the majority of the judges. They seemed to be thinking of the institutional uses of film, rather than film as art. Judgments were drawn from the fields of ethics and church polity rather than those inherent in the art.

Curiously enough, the Oscars presented by the Annual Motion Picture Academy were hardly more perceptive, especially the major awards such as the Best Picture, etc. These awards, coming from within the film industry, have depended more on box office success and the popularity of the principal actors, directors and producers than with anything to do with the art. The film industry was no more successful in resisting criteria of judgment drawn from other areas than the film itself than were the churches. Ironically, the religious awards recovered from their anti-art posture long before the industry. In fact, it looks as if the film industry will go on making primary evaluations on economic considerations, with occasional sentimental lapses to honor some particularly loved member of the commercial film community.

Most film criticism has been based on essentially literary criteria with judgments made from dramatic and moral premises. That is, films have been given "good" or "bad" marks because they succeeded or failed at hanging together in terms of essentially literary categories (plot, character realization, time-place unities, etc.) and their level of moral accomplishment (providing exemplary models for youth, satisfying community behavior codes, responding to patriotic

themes, etc.). For example, Antonioni's *Blow-Up* was generally considered to lack unity because the plot did not seem to go anywhere. It lacked the logical continuity of good narrative. While it was generally conceded that the mod photographer was well developed by David Hemning's acting, his lack of moral purpose was ethically repugnant. One critic noted pubic hair in a comic scene, which made it impossible, he said, to give the film anything but a failing mark.

Between the release of *Blow-Up,* late in 1966, and the appearance of *Easy Rider* two and one-half years later, many attitudes of what was permissible in commercial film changed, but there was not much alteration in the criticism. In terms of narrative development, *Easy Rider* was easier to handle than *Blow-Up.* It was patterned upon a venerable if minor novel form, the picaresque. While the critics acknowledged that the characters did seem to grab the under-30 generation (as did those of *Blow-Up),* they were morally indefensible for their involvement with drugs and their casual indifference to exemplary behavior. Altogether it was considered a rather dismal film. While it was generally conceded that *Blow-Up* was technically superb in its camera work, its use of color (even if it was over intense), the sound quality, the movement, *Easy Rider* was not given comparable scores. When compared with Antonioni's technical facility and precision, *Easy Rider* is sloppy. In the classic tradition, if the natural setting of street or park did not meet Antonioni's specifications, then he improved upon it. *Easy Rider*'s cameras take what they find, without worrying too much about light refraction on camera lenses or dust and grime.

Such evaluations, however, are not what is meant by knowing films in relation to their technology. It is not, basically, either facility or sloppiness in handling gadgets, sets, or the sound. It is the realization that the only way to know films is in the interraction of the images with the producing instruments. We do not want to put films back into the old slot which was for so long a hindrance to the development of painting and sculpture, *viz.,* evaluation based essentially on craftsmanship. It does, however, make an essential difference in the *character* of films when the cameraman is freed from the ponderous studio equipment, moved about on cumbersome

from Hopper's *Easy Rider*

dollies so that he can move into any crowd or place with his hand-held equipment which will give him just as good quality results as the studio equipment. The results are of a different *quality* when projections are made on the entire environment that surrounds the viewer, rather than on a little screen placed on a stage at one end of an auditorium, essentially the old proscenium character of drama which the new drama has been so frantically trying to escape. The mixture of color, movement and space is altered radically in perspectives and feelings of participation as all the senses (touch, smell, taste, as well as seeing and hearing) are activated.

The interpenetration of television technology with that of film is just barely scraping the surface. Films produced in relation to visual tape have a stupendous kind of visual gadgetry available. They are mostly geared wrong, but when the gauges start going crazy fantastic results are possible; things impossible for the straight film-lens exposure. It is almost at the opposite end of Warhol's funky use of his equipment. Warhol, in the sloppy use of his cameras and other equipment, has done a great thing for films' simplicity. The fantastic electronic gadgetry in a first class television studio, freed from the confines of formula production, will alter the possibilities of the movies' complexity.

Film criticism needs less dependence upon literary sources. As an alternative, the approaches of the visual arts in the last century are much more fruitful. The battle in painting and sculpture to free itself of the ancient adage that art is an "imitation of nature" has long since been won, but seems still to dominate films. Some how or other, naturalistic verism is still claimed as a "good" in cinema. There are yet many lessons that the contemporary artists have mastered that can make solid contributions to film.

Film, however, is able to move the visual arts into realms impossible for easel painting or sculpting. It has, therefore, engaged much interest for artists trained in studio painting. Film's use of the scenario, rather than the script, should have been exploited as an artistic model much more than it has. Unfortunately, most film-makers still treat the scenario as if it were a script. That is, their end results have been as if they were using the script continuity rather than the simultaneities implied in the scenario. Antonioni's

Blow-Up, for example, was faulted by many because of its scenario structure rather than the script. The history of movies had been disposed more toward the dramatic script than the filmic continuity.

All of these aspects: the awareness of the image through an electric and electronic technology, the exploitation of the essentially visual lessons of twentieth century art while at the same time opening up the rest of the senses to awareness and stimulation, the happening, or scenario continuity, the interpenetration of the creative process with the seeing public are the essentials of process criticism. These elements are shifting radically our realization of film as art. They result less in "good" and "bad" evaluations than in comments and contributions to the process of film realization. Clarity is realized less as generalized summaries than as involvement in film experience. The extent to which we can attain clarity is furnished by the ability by which we can orient ourselves anew to process.

Film art is an expansion of human experience. It is accomplished in the interplay between man and man, and man and nature. The procedure of film experience transforms, even as it changes human experience. It must not be conformed to predetermined "standards," but freed to move.

It is as religion. For human beings it seems always to have existed, but with every era it must be redone. Religion frozen is God dead. It is integral to human experience. And so are the ways of knowing, of illumination, of realization. These are the arenas of film art today.

94   72   963